Flexible Learning in Action

Case Studies in Higher Education

EDITED BY
RACHEL HUDSON
SIAN MASLIN-PROTHERO
LYN OATES

KOGAN PAGE

Published in association with the
Staff and Educational Development Association

The Staff and Educational Development Series
Series Editor: Sally Brown

Assessing Competence in Higher Education, edited by Anne Edwards and Peter Knight
Assessment for Learning in Higher Education, edited by Peter Knight
Enabling Student Learning: Systems and Strategies, edited by Gina Wisker and Sally Brown
Facing up to Radical Changes in Universities and Colleges, edited by Steve Armstrong, Gail Thompson and Sally Brown
Flexible Learning in Action: Case Studies in Higher Education, edited by Rachel Hudson, Sian Maslin-Prothero and Lyn Oates
The Management of Independent Learning, edited by Jo Tait and Peter Knight
Research, Teaching and Learning in Higher Education, edited by Brenda Smith and Sally Brown
Resource-Based Learning, edited by Sally Brown and Brenda Smith

First published in 1997

Kogan Page Limited
120 Pentonville Road
London N1 9JN

British Library Cataloguing in Publication Data

A CIP record for this book is available from the British Library.

ISBN 0 7494 2391 9

Typeset by Kogan Page Ltd
Printed and bound in Great Britain by Clays Ltd, St Ives plc

Contents

The Editors

Rachel Hudson, Open Learning Facilitator, Faculty of the Built Environment, University of the West of England, Bristol, England

Sian Maslin-Prothero, Lecturer, Department of Nursing and Midwifery Studies, Nottingham University, Nottingham, England

Lyn Oates, Learning and Teaching Support Manager, Cheltenham and Gloucester College of Higher Education, Cheltenham, England

The Contributors

Sally Anderson, Flexible Learning Manager, Education Development Unit, Napier University, Edinburgh, Scotland

Phil Askham, Senior Lecturer, School of Urban and Regional Studies, Sheffield Hallam University, Sheffield, England

Clare Bainbridge, Engineering Subject Librarian, University of the West of England, Bristol, England

Philip Barker, Professor of Applied Computing, School of Computing and Mathematics, University of Teeside, Middlesbrough, England

Rosie Bingham, Regular Visiting Lecturer, Learning and Teaching Institute/School of Education, Sheffield Hallam University, Sheffield, England

Don Bratton, Principal Lecturer, Department of Chemistry, University of Central Lancashire, Preston, England

Helen Breen, Academic Co-ordinator, Centre for Professional Development in Club Management, Southern Cross University, Lismore, New South Wales, Australia

Kathy Buckner, Lecturer, Department of Communication and Information Studies, Queen Margaret College, Edinburgh, Scotland

Tony Cavanagh, Document Delivery Librarian, Deakin University, Geelong, Victoria, Australia

Sybil Cock, Maths Learning Development and Support, Department of Higher Education and Access Development, University of North London, England

Maggie Challis, Senior Lecturer, Learning and Teaching Institute, Sheffield Hallam University, Sheffield, England

Elisabeth Davenport, Senior Lecturer, Department of Communication and Information Studies, Queen Margaret College, Edinburgh, Scotland

David Davies, Director, Continuing Education Unit, School of Continuing and Professional Education, University of Surrey, Guildford, England

Sue Drew, Senior Lecturer, Learning and Teaching Institute, Sheffield Hallam University, Sheffield, England

Lesley Dunning, Senior Lecturer in Education Studies, School of Education, University of Wolverhampton, Walsall, England

Stephen Fallows, Head of Educational Services Unit and Reader in Educational Development, Educational Services Unit, University of Luton, England

Robert Fulkerth, Assistant Professor, School of Technology and Industry, Golden Gate University, San Francisco, California, United States of America

Philip Garner, Senior Lecturer in Special Education, School of Education, Brunel University, Twickenham, England

Philip Gillies-Denning, Access Programme Manager, Centre for Learning and Teaching, Queen Margaret College, Edinburgh, Scotland

Maggie Grundy, Macmillan Lecturer in Cancer Nursing, Associate Faculty of Nursing, Midwifery and Community Studies, The Robert Gordon University, Aberdeen, Scotland

Keith Haddon, Information Officer, Library and Learning Resource Services, University of Central Lancashire, Preston, England

Nerilee Hing, Lecturer, School of Tourism and Hospitality Management, Southern Cross University, Lismore, New South Wales, Australia

Cathy Hole, Staff Development Adviser, Department of Staff Development, University of Bristol, England

Sally Lawton, Lecturer in Nursing, Associate Faculty of Nursing, Midwifery and Community Studies, The Robert Gordon University, Aberdeen, Scotland

Christopher Longman, Director, Academic and Professional Development Courses, School of Education, Brunel University, Twickenham, England

Martin Löschmann, Reader in Applied German Language, Department of Languages, Kingston University, Kingston-upon-Thames, England

William Lynch, Associate Professor and Director of Distance Learning, Department of Educational Leadership, The George Washington University, Washington DC, United States of America

William Macauley, Teaching Associate, Department of English, Indiana University of Pennsylvania, United States of America

Karen McArdle, Scheme Director, BA in Professional Development, Department of Community and Continuing Education, Northern College, Dundee, Scotland

Andrina McCormack, Senior Lecturer/DASET Programme Director, Department of Educational Studies, Northern College, Dundee, Scotland

Patrick McGhee, Associate Dean, Faculty of Arts, Sciences and Education, Bolton Institute, Bolton, England

Ian McGowan, Head of Department of Community and Continuing Education, Northern College, Dundee, Scotland

Susanne Mühlhaus, Teaching and Research Assistant, Department of Languages, Kingston University, Kingston-upon-Thames, England

David Oldroyd, Senior Lecturer, Department of Education, University of Bristol, England

Gian Pagnucci, Assistant Professor, Department of English, Indiana University of Pennsylvania, United States of America

Poppy Pickard, Lecturer in Mathematics and Computing, School of Mathematical Sciences, University of North London, England

Jackie Robinson, Manager of Flexible Learning Services, Stockport College of Further and Higher Education, Stockport, England

Lyn Shipway, Teaching and Learning Adviser, School of Advanced Nursing, Midwifery and Interprofessional Health Studies, Anglia Polytechnic University, Brentwood, England

Chris Smith, Senior Lecturer, Department of Psychology, University of Central Lancashire, Preston, England

Edward Smith, Head of the Centre for Learning Technologies, University of Central Lancashire, Preston, England

Richard Steward, Computer Consultant, Henley-on-Thames, England

Armida Taylor, Course Leader BA in Nursing/BA in Community Nursing, School of Nursing, The Robert Gordon University, Aberdeen, Scotland

Jenny Ure, Development Officer, Centre for Continuing Education, University of Aberdeen, Aberdeen, Scotland

Winnie Wade, Flexible Learning Co-ordinator, Flexible Learning Initiative, Loughborough University, Loughborough, England

Paul Weeks, Lecturer, School of Tourism and Hospitality Management, Southern Cross University, Lismore, New South Wales, Australia

Angus Witherby, Senior Lecturer, Department of Geography and Planning, University of New England, Armidale, New South Wales, Australia

Introduction

Rachel Hudson, Sian Maslin-Prothero and Lyn Oates

WHY THIS EDITED COLLECTION?

This publication originates from a piece of research supported by the Staff and Educational Development Association (SEDA) which investigated the need for staff involved with flexible learning initiatives in higher education to network with each other (Campbell and Hudson 1995). The research revealed a wealth of innovative developments taking place in a wide range of subject disciplines and central services. Since staff from such a diverse range of areas would not normally have the opportunity to meet, this led to the formation of the SEDA Flexible Learning Network, which has the aims of sharing ideas, problems and best practice in flexible learning in higher education across the United Kingdom. In order to promote its aims, the Network formed an electronic discussion group, flexible-learning@mailbase.ac.uk. Similar electronic discussion groups have formed around distance learning in the United States of America (deosl@lists.psu.edu) and the Open and Distance Learning Association of Australia (resodlaa@usq.edu.au). The case studies in this book are drawn from the experiences of members of these three networks and are intended to reflect the diversity of approaches to incorporating flexibility in course design and delivery. The variety of responses detailed in these case studies also underlines the fact that there is no one way to provide flexible learning and that there is no single agreed definition.

STUDENT-CENTRED, TEACHER-CENTRED OR BOTH?

There is a confusion in the minds of practitioners between the terms open, distance, flexible and resource-based learning, which the literature compounds. Often they are used inter-changeably, sometimes one subsumes the other:

The *A–Z of Open Learning* (Jeffries, Lewis, Meed and Merritt, 1990) highlights the problem: 'Flexible learning. This term has no universally accepted definition. It is perhaps best used to describe forms of education and training which have sought to become more open by responding to the specific needs (eg for materials, support or assessment) and aspirations of individual learners' (p.48).

The *Open Learning Handbook* (Race 1994) also refers to the problems of terminology: 'In some ways... "flexible learning" is the most satisfactory of the three terms [open, distance and flexible learning]. Both "open learning" in its broadest sense, and "distance learning" as a sub-set of open learning, involve giving learners some degree of choice and control. In other words, they introduce elements of flexibility into the learning process' (p.22).

In an unpublished paper, *Open Learning in Higher Education*, Roger Lewis reviews a number of innovations in higher education. He states that some of these studies prefer to use other terms such as resource-based learning, independent learning, self-managed learning and flexible learning. However, he concludes that: 'When defined broadly – as the provision of greater student access to, and choice over, learning – the term "open learning" acceptably covers all the cases described.'

In addition, the literature tends to define flexible learning both in terms of the elements of flexibility needed by students (ie from a student-centred perspective) and from the dimensions of flexibility to be provided (ie from a teacher- or institution-centred perspective). For example, Wade, (1994) defines flexible learning mainly in student-centred terms: 'Flexible learning... is an approach to university education which provides students with the opportunity to take greater *responsibility* for their learning and to be engaged in learning activities and opportunities that meet their own individual needs' (p.12).

MacFarlene (1992) takes a more teacher-centred approach: 'The term [flexible learning] has been used as a banner under which to promote a shift from formal, whole-class didactic teaching towards individual or group management of learning through the provision, by the teacher, of structured resource materials, together with opportunities for the negotiation of tasks (often through specific "learning contracts" drawn up to formalize requirements for the individual), self- and peer-assessment, and collaborative group work, often on "real-life" projects' (p.5).

Thomas (1995) proposes a model for flexible learning which focuses on the dynamics of the learning process which take place between the expert, the learner and the learning resource. In this model the needs of the learner are just one of many elements which determine the dynamics of the learning process.

ELEMENTS OF FLEXIBILITY

When we started collecting case studies for this book, we were looking to illustrate our view that flexible learning is essentially student-centred learning, and is about meeting student needs using whatever methods of teaching and learning are most appropriate. At the same time, we wished to dispel the commonly held view that flexible learning is concerned mainly with the use of specially prepared resource-based learning materials designed to replace tutor contact.

The brief for authors stated that we were looking for case studies which were aimed at improving access, giving students control and choice over what and how they learned, helping them take responsibility for their learning, and providing support appropriate to individual learner's needs. These four elements:

- access;
- control;
- responsibility;
- support.

were identified as the key concepts underpinning flexible learning in a piece of cross-sectoral research conducted by the Scottish Council for Educational Technology (1993).

Not surprisingly, while emphasing these important elements, the case studies described initiatives from both student-centred and teacher- or institution-centred perspectives. While they all had clear learning objectives and had been evaluated in terms of learning success, they also illustrated responses to a range of external drivers pushing for greater flexibility in course design and delivery.

DRIVERS FOR FLEXIBILITY IN HIGHER EDUCATION

Until this point, we had held the view that since flexible learning is about meeting student needs, the main drivers behind the increasing interest in flexible learning in higher education would be related to changes in the student body. Our case studies revealed a more complex picture.

Pedagogy

The majority of case studies illustrate how lecturers have introduced greater flexibility in order to improve the quality of the student learning experience. Their aims have been to promote greater active learning, more experiential learning and to encourage reflective learning.

Cuts in funding

Higher education is experimenting with a number of different teaching and learning methods at the moment, many of them driven by the need to be more resource efficient. There is a general belief that offering students greater choice through modularity and encouraging them to take greater responsibility for their learning are both initiatives motivated as much by resource constraints as by the desire to meet student needs. In addition, greater flexibility in course delivery is being introduced in a bid to find new markets and so increase or maintain income.

Increasing diversity of students

Tremendous changes have taken place in the student population, and these have been charted in the recently published Institute for Employment Studies (IES) Report (Connor 1996). In the ten years preceding 1993/4, the number of people entering full-time higher education in the United Kingdom has increased by over 76 per cent. However, it is not just the increase in student numbers, but also the increasing diversity of students which has led to the need for greater flexibility.

There is now a broader range of acceptable entry qualifications for higher education and this has implications for the skills that students bring with them. One third of full-time first degree students enter with qualifications other than 'A' levels or Highers (Connor 1996). While school leavers remain a significant proportion of higher education recruits, they arrive with different learning experiences. Some will arrive with good information technology skills, often familiar with applications that are more up-to-date than those on the student computer network – but these new skills may have been learned at the expense of others. There was a 203 per cent increase in the number of mature students (25 +) entering higher education between 1988/9 and 1993/4 (Connor 1996). They differ from the school leaver by usually having experience of work (sometimes at a managerial level), of raising a family and having good time-management skills. It is clear from this description that the individual members of a class of the late 1990s will have very different approaches to study. They will need targeted support to help them build on their different strengths and overcome their different weaknesses, and the opportunity to negotiate a programme of studies that meet their varied personal and professional development needs.

Today, many students have to juggle their studies with other major commitments. The cuts in student grants means that many full-time students have to find part-time employment and have reduced choice about where they go to university. Mature students often have dependent relatives to care for, and may continue to hold down a permanent job while studying part-time. Higher education courses need to be more flexible to help students cope with so many conflicting demands on their time. Students need more choice over the time, place and pace of their studies.

Equal opportunities

The demand for flexibility is seemingly endless. The IES Report (Connor 1996) reveals that the current student body does not reflect the diversity of society as a whole. Most higher education institutions have equal opportunity policy statements committing themselves to improving access to their programmes. If these policies are to be implemented, courses will need to be designed and delivered in ways which meet the needs of all potential students, including those with disabilities, those from different ethnic cultures, residents of remote areas, shift workers, those who work in varying locations, and those who need to make one or more mid-life career changes, and so on.

Labour market requirements

Students are changing, funding is changing, and so are the requirements of the labour market. Everyone is expected to continually update their knowledge and skills. No one expects a job for life. The aim of the European Year of Lifelong Learning (1996) was to raise awareness regarding the concept of lifelong learning and to develop initiatives at local, national and international levels (European Commission [EC] 1995). The emphasis of the EC is on the role of education and training in developing lifelong learning. The EC's accent is on lifelong education.

Transferable skills

Students need to be employable. The rapid pace of change has meant that employers have pushed for a change in emphasis from 'knowledge' to the development of the skills of the 'knower' so that companies can become more innovative and flexible and can act effectively in a changing world. Organizations are now seeking a multi-skilled, responsive and adaptable workforce who are prepared to be lifelong learners, adapting and changing as required by the organization (English National Board 1994). Since the concept of a job for life no longer exists, so people need to be self-motivated and make conscious decisions about their futures.

STRUCTURE OF THE BOOK

This book has been structured to show the diversity of initiatives that are taking place in higher education in response to the drivers outlined above.

Flexibility for learners on campus

The majority of students in higher education are 'campus-based'. The case studies in this section illustrate a range of ways in which greater flexibility is being offered to these students. Most describe flexible developments which are taking place at a module or unit level. For example, computer-assisted learning packages, e-mail and resource-based learning materials are being used to give students more choice about when and where they learn. Students are being offered choice in their assessment schedule, and in one example, can select a 'judicious mix' of self-study materials, lectures, tutorials and seminars. Several of the case studies involve the use of technologies such as the World Wide Web, computer conferencing and e-mail to give students greater flexibility over when and where they study. While many students are still using the universities' computing facilities to take part in these modules, several have been able to communicate from home.

Flexibility for work-based learners

Perhaps because the case studies in this section are concerned with students who are identifiably different from 'traditional' full-time students, they take a more student-centred approach. These case studies refer to the need for negotiated learning to ensure relevance to the students' working situation; the need to build in reflection-on-practice and experiential learning; and to the development of assessment methods such as portfolios and profiling to aid reflective learning and professional and personal development.

Flexible approaches to skills development

The case studies in this section illustrate a range of flexible modes of delivery adopted by higher education institutions in order to meet the challenge of developing students' transferable skills and skills for lifelong learning. For example, the use of handbooks and tutorials to ensure that postgraduates can make effective use of campus computer facilities for research; the development of a wide range of resource-based learning materials for a campus-wide programme aimed at developing effective learning skills. The case studies also illustrate ways of identifying and overcoming barriers to lifelong learning. For example, by establishing partnerships with the community from which the learners are drawn; by including confidence building activities; and by establishing a range of mechanisms to ensure appropriate support, including mentors, drop-in sessions and student networks.

Institutional strategies for supporting flexible learning

Several of the case studies in this section concern initiatives which have been supported because the institution wishes to learn more about the benefits of 'new' teaching and learning methods, perhaps in the hope that they will help them cope with reduced contact time. Nevertheless, the emphasis of most case studies, while not being wholly student-centred, is essentially on meeting the needs of students. Thus, the final section, on institutional strategies, describes a series of initiatives to provide a framework in which flexible learning can take place, and reflects the importance which higher education is placing on flexible learning. The case studies include examples of a mixed-mode modular programme, local and remote access to electronic learning resources, and an institution-wide strategy for learning skills development.

REFERENCES

Campbell, F and Hudson, R (1995) 'Flexible Learning in Higher Education: Effective Methods of Staff Networking', in: Percival, F; Land, R and Edgar-Nevill (eds) (1995) *Aspects of Education and Training Technology XXVIII: Computer Assisted and Open Access Education*, Kogan Page, London

Connor, H *et al.*, (1996) *University Challenge, Student Choices in the Twenty-first Century*, IES Report no. 306, Institute for Employment Studies, Brighton

European Commission (1995) *European Year of Lifelong Learning. Guidelines*, European Commission, Brussels

English National Board for Nursing, Midwifery and Health Visiting (1994) 'Creating Lifelong Learners: Partnerships for Care'. *Guidelines for the Implementation of the United Kingdom Central Council Standards for Education and Practice Following Registration*, ENB, London

Jeffries, C; Lewis, R; Meed, J and Merritt, R (1990) *The A-Z of Open Learning*, National Extension College, Cambridge

Lewis, R (1996) *Open Learning in Higher Education*, Unpublished

MacFarlene, A (1992) *Teaching and Learning in an Expanding Higher Education System*, The Committee of Scottish University Principals, Edinburgh

Race, P (1994) *Open Learning Handbook – Promoting Quality in Designing and Delivering Flexible Learning*, Kogan Page, London

Scottish Centre for Educational Technology (1993) *The Co-ordination of Flexible Learning in Scotland – A Cross Sectoral Perspective*, SCET, Glasgow

Thomas, D (1995) *Flexible Learning Strategies in Higher and Further Education*, Cassell, London

Wade, W; Hodgkinson, K; Smith, A and Arfield, J (eds) (1994) *Flexible Learning in Higher Education*, Kogan Page, London

SECTION I
Flexibility for Learners on Campus

INTRODUCTION

Since the majority of students in higher education attend a univerisity campus for many of their learning activities, this section features a number of case studies designed to introduce greater flexibility into campus-based learning. All the case studies involve no more than a single unit or module – sometimes less – so it is probably fair to assume that in the majority of cases the students' overall learning experience remains much less flexible.

In most cases, the modules or units featured have been taught on previous occasions, using more conventional methods, but a range of factors have led to a shift away from traditional patterns of learning and to the introduction of greater flexibility. All the changes were introduced with the aim of improving the quality of the learning experience and being more responsive to student needs. For example, peer-assisted study sessions were introduced to try to overcome high failure rates and help students develop effective learning strategies (Witherby, Chapter 4). In another case (Dunning, Chapter 2), it seemed 'bizarre' to lecture about flexible learning. Sometimes the need for greater flexibility arose because of the changing nature of the students, for example, independent learning strategies were introduced because students with very different language abilities selected the same language module (Mühlhaus and Löschmann, Chapter 3).

Most of the case studies aim to give students greater control over the time, pace and place of their studies. They also aim to give students greater control and choice over what and how they learn, often by giving them access to a wide range of learning materials and helping them to develop effective learning skills. Some of the benefits of increased flexibility have been extended to staff – for example, the introduction of e-mail has meant that lecturers can choose the time when they respond to student queries (Smith, Chapter 5).

Several case studies clearly have some experimental aspect to them – the departments or institutions wish to learn more about the benefits of these new methods of delivery: whether greater flexibility will enable them to recruit more overseas students (Dunning, Chapter 2) or whether multimedia is an effective method of teaching (Smith *et al.*, Chapter 7).

While some of the case studies make clear reference to diminished resources as a driver for change (e-mail 'came to the rescue' when there were no available rooms or staff to teach 72 psychology students (Smith, Chapter 5) and 'the few contact hours now available' for the language module could no longer be used for teaching content (Mühlhaus and Löschmann, Chapter 3)), most are less specific. In almost all the case studies it seems that in order to introduce greater flexibility, resources have been redeployed rather than reduced. The lecturers' time has been spent developing learning materials, running workshops to improve students' learning strategies, responding to e-mail queries, and marking reflective journals, rather than on transmitting content via lectures.

Increased flexibility for students has led to a change in the role of the lecturer. By giving students more control over when, where, what and how they learn, lecturers are spending less time presenting information, and more time as learning facilitators: progress checking, motivating students, developing students' learning strategies, establishing peer support, holding 'remedial' workshops or lectures in response to student problems.

In all the case studies, the overall timescale for studying the module remains inflexible, and much of the assessment remains non-negotiable. It seems likely that the constraints of organizing a modular programme for full-time students are responsible for this lack of flexibility. Dunning (Chapter 2) states that students welcomed the fixed timescale and clear direction regarding the assessment.

In several case studies, increased flexibility has been offered by the use of e-mail, computer conferencing and the World Wide Web, for example Buckner and Davenport (Chapter 6). As students gain access to the Internet, this will mean that essentially campus-based students now have the opportunity to study almost an entire module from home. This could eventually lead to the blurring of the distinction between 'campus-based' and 'distance' learners. However, as the online 'Business Writing' course shows (Fulkerth, Chapter 1), many students do not have access to computers or the Internet at home, and must rely on using the computer labs on the university campus.

Chapter 1

Teaching Business Writing Online: Towards Developing Student Learning and Responsibility in a Flexible Learning Environment

Robert Fulkerth

This case study describes an online business writing course taught in an electronic bulletin board environment. The course, 'English 120: Advanced Business Writing', is a core course in the undergraduate curriculum and has been taught in the traditional format by teachers for many years; I have been teaching it at least twice a year since 1991. Class size varies between 10 and 20, depending on teacher, time of day, and semester. The students are of three types: adult working professionals, international students, and a smaller number of traditional American college students.

INTRODUCTION

Designing flexible yet substantive online courses for this diverse group is challenging, particularly in the area of business writing. Contemporary writing pedagogy calls for high-interaction activities such as peer editing and multiple reviews of works-in-progress; for many second language students, more direct intervention is often necessary. Overall, online courses are popular, but this course is unique in that it is a school-wide requirement, so it is expected that enrolment will continue to grow. In 1996, I offered the course online, and enrolment was seven. The second time it was offered, 23 students enrolled, but the class size was capped at 20. The course will again be offered, this time using Internet conferencing tools, during the Fall of 1997.

SETTING

The emergence of online education has impacted upon Golden Gate University, much as it has on other private institutions. The University's seven California sites (with programme offerings in Samoa and Malaysia) offer undergraduate through to doctoral degrees in information systems, business, law, finance, taxation, liberal studies and public service, in highly competitive urban market environments. Reduced enrolments resulting from restructuring in the business community and dwindling employer financial support, as well as competition from other institutions, have created a need to reach new student populations by innovations in programme delivery.

One result is that instructors from various disciplines are now offering online courses. These are taught in a variety of formats, such as real-time audio-video, bulletin boards/e-mail, and via the Internet/World Wide Web. These offerings have evolved in the absence of direct institutional support, although as this is written an entity called Cybercampus has been formed to serve as an umbrella for some online offerings.

HYPOTHESIS

'Advanced Business Writing' is a junior level course that most students must take to complete Golden Gate University's undergraduate degree programmes. Thus, students described in this case study reflect the make-up of our overall student body: 60 per cent adult working professionals, 30 per cent international students, and a relatively fewer number (10 per cent) of 'traditional' American college students.

My initial belief was that it is not possible to teach an effective writing course online, to a diverse group of students, in an e-mail/bulletin board environment. I suspected that it would be little more than an electronic correspondence course. None the less, I set out to create an effective course, satisfying to students, whose learning outcomes would be defensible within the institution and to the University's accrediting body.

RESEARCH RATIONALE

Electronically mediated instruction calls into focus the tension between traditional pedagogies and those that address the electronic learning space. In configuring the online class, I relied on Knowles' (1984) theories of the adult learner, characterized as andragogy, which posit that adults have particular learning characteristics that challenge traditional pedagogical models. These students are characterized as self-directing, experienced, motivated and ready to learn; they learn best via educational strategies that draw on those characteristics.

In the face-to-face classroom, classroom assessment activities (Angelo and Cross, 1993) have proved highly useful for gathering course-related and personal information from students that might otherwise be unavailable. Various assessment activities were used in the online 'Advanced Business Writing' course, to gather 'just in time' information about coursework and student concerns.

Some contemporary composition pedagogies expect that students will interact in peer editing groups around draft versions of writings in progress. Electronic groups are therefore a major feature of the online course. Student feedback in face-to-face classes suggest that students learn to value the input of peers, if the input is structured and is seen as supportive. A comprehensive discussion of group interaction in the online environment is found in Eastmond (1995). In an attempt to emulate components of traditional group processes found to be effective, my online students were placed in groups, provided with evaluation criteria, and were expected to interact regularly with each other's letter assignments.

RESEARCH QUESTIONS

Providing online education challenges institutions themselves, but at the course level, more interesting challenges occur for teachers. How do instructors configure substantive online courses that address the flexibility promised by online education?

Given the high expectations of today's students (and the high tuition fees they pay), how do teachers ensure quality online instruction while addressing differences in students' academic and personal backgrounds and skills, and their varied access to and expertise with technology? Perhaps most important, how do students achieve in an electronic environment compared with their achievement on traditional courses?

STRUCTURE OF THE ONLINE ADVANCED BUSINESS WRITING CLASS

When students enter the English 120 course, they see a number of folders for different activities, such as weekly assignments, hints for success in online classes, classmate biographies, and group folders. Folders are open to all with the exception of the group folders, which are limited to students in a particular group and the instructor. Students enter appropriate folders to find the syllabus, weekly assignments and contact information about other students. It is through this window that they post responses to other members of their particular group.

Course materials are highly structured as to expectations and due dates. Mini-lectures direct students to text materials, and they complete regular quizzes that are submitted via e-mail. Letter writing and a research proposal assignment form the bulk of the course work, although a midterm examination is set to address concerns of plagiarism, and to allow the instructor to meet those students who take the course on the San Francisco campus.

GROUP INTERACTIONS ONLINE: LETTER ASSIGNMENTS

Students interact in groups to discuss and edit the letter assignments. These assignments cover a three week period, during which students receive an assignment, submit a draft to the group folder, interact with other members' drafts, edit according to group members' suggestions, and submit a final version via fax to the instructor. The final letter is evaluated and returned by surface mail to students within three days of the submission date.

THE RESEARCH PROPOSAL

The major assignment of the course is a research proposal that attempts to solve a specific problem encountered in the students' work environment. This assignment carries a substantial number of points and completion is required to receive credit for the course. There are a number of checkpoints and discussions about the paper as it progresses during the trimester, many of which are carried on via e-mail. A formal draft is submitted during the eleventh week, and the instructor and student then conference via phone or e-mail to discuss the paper.

The course is designed around a simulation in which students and the instructor work for the hypothetical XZY Corporation, so a student can 'work' in an area that reflects his or her real job. If the student does not work in real life, he or she can choose a generic job that reflects the student's interest. Thus, topics for the research proposal reflect contemporary business matters such as choosing a business database, using e-mail effectively or introducing a new product in the marketplace. In addition to researching a topic, students are expected to place the topic within a persuasive proposal.

FINDINGS

Based on the experience of teaching this course many times in the face-to-face format and twice in the electronic format, I now believe that it is possible to successfully teach a writing course online to adult students. Learning outcomes in the online course can match those of the face-to-face course, if several considerations are addressed:

- Course design must consider the nature of the electronic learning space and the online instructional medium.
- Grading criteria must be clear and consistently applied.
- The course must be highly organized.
- Expectations must be high, yet attainable. They should match those of the face-to-face course.
- There must be an avenue for active discussion among students/students and student/teacher. In addition to providing a generally positive communicative environment, this enables students of different skill, talent and interest levels to have their needs addressed.
- Feedback on coursework must be personalized, timely and substantive.
- A variety of technologies should be used; the telephone is valuable.

The online environment changes the role of the teacher from dispenser of information to disseminator and director of the course experience. The primary focus becomes the students' outcomes rather than the teacher's input. Students can feel empowered as they direct their own activities, ask for and receive help from their classmates, and interpret course material for themselves.

However, online courses are not for all students. Those who have English language difficulties must seek tutorial or writing centre help. A second factor is access. Some students do not have the necessary access to computer technology, choosing instead to do their work in computer labs during their time on campus. Finally, students who are not able to work alone or who are not highly motivated towards completion will fall by the wayside, and will require much of the instructor's time.

CONCLUSION

Assessments show that 82 per cent of students feel that 'the course is comparable to or better than' a traditional face-to-face course. In a final course assessment, one student wrote, 'I was pleasantly surprised. I thought I wrote pretty well because I write all the time at work, but the assignments made me pay attention to my writing all over again. Plus, I got to do the work after my kids (and husband) went to bed.'

Enrolments in our school's online courses are growing. Ease of access and the flexibility of the electronic environment seem to be key features that draw our students online. Many discover, as did the student above, that the online environment makes them more directly responsible for their learning outcomes, and they rise to the challenge. Well-taught online courses can complement our students' lives, learning styles, and educational needs.

REFERENCES

Angelo, T and Cross, P (1993) *Classroom assessment techniques: A handbook for college teachers* Jossey Bass Inc., San Francisco

Eastmond, D (1995) *Alone but together: Adult distance study through computer conferencing* Hampton Press Inc., Cresskill, New Jersey

Knowles, M S and associates (1984) *Andragogy in Action*, Jossey Bass Inc, San Francisco

Chapter 2

Don't Lecture Me about Flexible Learning! Being Flexible in the Delivery of an Undergraduate Education Studies Module

Lesley Dunning

The University of Wolverhampton offers Education Studies as a subject in its modular undergraduate programme; students study four modules over a period of 15 weeks (one semester). Each module generates 45 hours' contact time and 105 hours' directed time. Contact time is, typically, interpreted as a programme of 12 or 14 lectures, often to large numbers of students, followed by seminar sessions for groups of up to 30 students, and one short individual tutorial. In 1995 a module 'Flexible Learning in Education and Training' was introduced into the portfolio. Twenty-six students opted for the module. Of these, almost half were mature students and two were studying part-time.

INTRODUCTION

The notion of lecturing to students about open and flexible modes of learning seemed somewhat bizarre; we wanted students to have first hand experience of some of the key concepts of the module. Our reasons for shifting away from the traditional pattern were educational, but they were commensurate with the needs of the School of Education to reassess the patterns of teaching and learning in the light of diminishing resources and diverse recruitment patterns. The lessons learned would clearly have implications within the School and for our growing overseas market, where traditional modes of delivery are becoming logistically problematic.

CONTENT AND TEACHING AND LEARNING METHODS

Students were required to demonstrate application and analysis of theoretical frameworks in the context of open and flexible learning, understand the recent developments in education and training which have precipitated flexible learning, and understand the contexts in which flexible learning is most appropriate. The module content was broken down into four study units. For each unit there was an introductory teaching session and a study guide consisting of interactive text written by staff, and accompanying source materials with directed reading tasks. At the end of each unit tutors were available to see students in small groups to discuss their progress and identify any weaknesses. Students were informed at the outset that they could choose to use the study units either in conjunction with the teaching sessions or instead of them, since the sessions covered the same material, but in a different way. They were, however, strongly advised to attend the tutorials.

The assessment of the module, with differentiated criteria for levels two and three (corresponding to year two and year three of an undergraduate programme of study) was less flexible. There was a set essay title with a 60 per cent weighting, and a choice of topic for each of two seminar papers worth 20 per cent each. Inevitably there were set deadlines for submission.

EVALUATION

Twenty-six students participated in the module. Of these, a third were mature students with occupational and family commitments, and two were part-time students attracted to the module by its flexible mode of delivery. Records of attendance were kept; roughly half the students, consistently the same group, availed themselves of all the contact time available, a quarter attended tutorials only and a quarter appeared only for the assessment seminars.

Data for the evaluation was collected through a detailed module experience questionnaire based on performance indicators adapted from Ramsden (1991) and focus group evaluations. We were also able to glean a lot about students' perceptions of flexible learning from the seminar papers presented as part of the assessment.

Our interest lay in two key areas: students' perception of the 'flexibility' of the module in the context of their personal needs, and the perceived quality of the learning experience.

The flexibility of the learning experience

Lewis (1994) reminds us that 'open' or 'flexible' learning offers enhanced choice of one or more aspects of the learning process, including time, place, pace, content, method, media, route and assessment methods. The constraints of the modular system precluded any flexibility with regard to pace and assessment methods. In any case, the majority of students asserted the value to them of a fixed time scale and a clear direction regarding assessment. The flexibility of time, place and mode of study brought mixed blessings; a few students felt the removal of any obligation as 'a relief', mainly because of family commitments, while others acknowledged that the flexibility provided a 'perfect excuse for not attending lectures'. Interestingly, at the end of the module some regret for this approach was expressed. As one focus group put it: 'in the end...those following the flexible route found that they had missed a lot by not attending lectures'. This could well be because, with a group of 26, the 'lecture' was in fact interactive and to some extent learner-centred; responses may have been different had there been a mass lecture programme.

Flexibility, then, lay in the choices students had with regard to *how* and *where* they studied. Whether they perceived choice with regard to *what* they studied depended upon the quality of the individual learning experience.

The quality of the learning experience

Most importantly, students found the flexible model 'very appropriate to the content of the module' since they were experiencing, at first hand, at least some of the conceptual frameworks of the module. Students' perceptions of the indicative content gave much food for thought. The large majority (78 per cent) agreed or strongly agreed that they felt encouraged to develop their own academic interests as far as possible and that the study units were a good starting point. One focus group commented that the study units 'gave us the opportunity to follow our own interests without worrying about missing important information'. Where students felt confident enough in the study units to explore related areas and undertake independent reading, we were encouraged that they seemed to be demonstrating the kind of 'deep' approaches to learning described by Ramsden (1992).

A few students acknowledged, however, that they had taken 'surface' approaches to their learning, recognizing that they 'got away' with studying the content of the study units only, exercising no other choice than to opt out of lectures and use the units as a 'prop' to see them through the assessments at the minimum level. These students tended to opt out of attendance altogether, whereas others saw the tutorial variously as 'invaluable', 'helpful' and 'informative and essential'. Indeed, the only comments received about how the module might be improved related to tutorials; students wanted more, they wanted them on demand, and they wanted them on a one-to-one basis. This is an interesting, though not unexpected paradox for a project with an agenda to examine ways of reducing tutor contact time.

CONCLUSION

The key areas of flexibility lay in place and mode of delivery; students were keenly aware that more of the responsibility for learning had been shifted in their direction, and that they had more control over how, where and when they learned. The flexible mode of delivery enabled them to synthesize personal experience with at least some of the conceptual frameworks of the module; they were able to compare the role of the learner as defined, for example, by Cuthbert (1994) with their own learning style, and those women who did not attend lectures simply because it made it easier to pick up the children from school understood Faith's point (1988, cited in Tait 1994) that open and distance learning 'colludes with traditional gender roles and expectations by facilitating women's confinement to the home' (p.34). Most importantly, all students experienced new demands made on themselves as learners, and the changing role of their tutors. As Parsons and Gibbs (1994) put it, the study units did the job of presenting information at least as well as conventional teaching, and that left tutors free to do the things which are 'more difficult to do in learning resources, such as discussion, negotiation, motivation and responding to individuals' (p.25).

Clearly some students coped better with the role shift than others, leading us to an all too familiar conclusion: that different students present different learning styles and that an eclectic approach is required to accommodate them.

What is evident from this small-scale research, however, is that the role of the tutor is pivotal to the success of any open, distance and flexible learning programme, and tutor time is an expensive resource. We are not, therefore, *reducing* tutor time by introducing flexible methods, but redeploying it. Flexible learning is not about replacing the teacher with another, increasingly more technological, medium. It is about optimizing current resources, and especially human resources, in order to meet the needs of an increasingly diverse group of students.

REFERENCES

Cuthbert, P (1994) 'Self-development groups on a Diploma in Management course' in: Thorley, L and Gregory, R (eds) *Using Group-Based Learning in Higher Education*, Kogan Page, London

Tait, A (1994) 'The End of Innocence: Critical approaches to Open and Distance Learning' *Open Learning* November, pp. 27–36

Lewis, R (1994) 'Speaking Up for Open Learning' *Adults Learning* March, pp. 173–4

Parsons, C and Gibbs, G (1994) *Course Design for Resource Based Learning: Education*, Oxford Centre for Staff Development, Oxford Brooks University, Oxford

Ramsden, P (1991) 'A Performance Indicator of Teaching Quality in Higher Education: the Course Experience Questionnaire' *Studies in Higher Education* 16:2 pp. 129–50

Ramsden, P (1992) *Learning to Teach in Higher Education*, Routledge, London

Chapter 3

Improving Independent Learning with Aural German Programmes

Susanne Mühlhaus and Martin Löschmann

The subjects of this study are full-time students of year one and year four language modules at Kingston University. This case study focuses on flexible learning approaches encouraged by German aural packages.

INTRODUCTION

The need for a more flexible approach to foreign language teaching at Kingston University has arisen largely due to institutional changes and more students. Since the modularization of many courses, students have been offered a greater choice of subjects, resulting in more students opting to study one or two languages in combination with another subject such as history or psychology. Students are now expected to enrol on individual modules and shape their own programme.

As students are recruited from the United Kingdom and abroad, including Erasmus and Socrates students, there are big differences concerning interests, background knowledge, learning experience, skills, language proficiency and socioeconomic factors.

Due to these factors a more flexible approach to the time and place of delivery was required. Components of some language modules for intermediate and advanced levels have since been offered in a workshop mode with between two and four tutor contact hours per semester. This choice was guided by the following criteria:

- avoiding time-consuming content teaching;
- enabling students to practise lifelong learning strategies and to be responsible for their own learning;
- generating effective conditions for self-directed learning;
- availability of learning resources outside the classroom.

The few contact hours now available can no longer be used for teaching content in all courses, and a distance learning approach has been adopted instead to maximize learning outcomes. Workshop time is now used to advise students on independent learning and to check their progress, while the learning activities take place outside the classroom.

AURAL PACKAGE AS THE BASIS OF WORKSHOPS

Although aural packages are used in years one, two and four, our case study concentrates on the aural component of year one and year four German. Since 1993 special aural packages have been used in foreign language teaching at Kingston University. In 1995 we completely revised these to make student learning more flexible. The aims of the aural packages are to develop and improve students' listening and summary skills of natural spoken German (including some regional varieties), to extend their vocabulary, register and knowledge of contemporary German language, and to develop lifelong learning strategies.

The materials used were radio and television broadcasts from various sources, including commercially produced language learning resources, such as 'BBC-Select' and 'Authentic'.

Each aural package consists of the following elements:

- A booklet which explains to the student the purpose of the programme, the aims and learning objectives, and tasks which students are asked to perform, model answer sheets and transcripts.
- A number of video and some audio clips (between four and seven per semester) of varying length (4-15 minutes).

Copies of the videos are available from the library, either for viewing on TV and video sets in a designated area (the language studio), or to take home and view at leisure. This facilitated access at a convenient time and place. Access was enhanced by choosing videos on topics which are both relevant and of interest to students. A clip about a driving school in Germany, for example, showed how different the process of obtaining a driving licence is in Germany. Other topics range from squatting in Potsdam to genetic engineering.

LEARNING ACTIVITIES

The activities students engage in when working through each unit of the programme are set out below. Although we know that no two students are the same, and the exact activities have to remain flexible according to different levels, our practice suggests that independent activities should normally follow this sequence for each unit:

- Completing a set of preparatory worksheets focusing on language structures and vocabulary which a particular video clip contains. Year four students engage in structured association exercises for anticipation of key content words of the video clip. An alternative way of preparation is using the silent screen first and noting down what could be going on in the video.

- Reading instructions for a guided summary with key points to look out for. For year four, not all key points are given, and students might ignore them as they feel they do not need them anymore.

- Viewing a video clip a set number of times. At the beginning we advise students to view videos several times, later on they are asked to reduce this number. In the final year they should be able to grasp the content by viewing only once.

- Writing a summary in English addressing certain key points.

- Evaluating their own summary according to a special marking scheme by comparing it with a model summary. Year four are required to see the model summary as an example only, and to compare it critically with their own work.

- Working through the transcript of the video with a dictionary to fill gaps and deepen understanding of difficult passages. In case of misunderstanding or failure to understand, students should translate the incomprehensible paragraph.

- Compiling a vocabulary list of their own choice and learning the vocabulary.

- Interacting with the materials, i.e. recording feelings about it (boring, interesting, and why), observations about how the topic or language relates to previous knowledge, how working through the transcript helps or otherwise, and specific comments about the learning process, strategies, outcomes, any difficulties, and thoughts about how to overcome these.

JOURNAL

As most of our students displayed a lack of learning strategies, we were looking for ways which might lead them to find more effective strategies. One of these was to keep a journal. Any work required on the student's part, including self-reflective comments, worksheet tasks, video summaries and vocabulary lists, were to be kept in the journal, which took any format the student was happy with, and had to be submitted periodically to the tutor. We devised a marking scheme to take into account the interaction with the material and the depth of the learning process, as evident from the students' vocabulary lists, translations and comments.

RELATIONSHIP BETWEEN CLASSROOM WORK AND OUT-OF-CLASSROOM LEARNING

When analysing students' journals, we found that some common learning issues emerged, such as viewing without any preparation, viewing more than four times, unstructured note-taking, looking most of the new words up in a dictionary, and listing them all without any context and grammatical characteristics.

These formed topics for subsequent workshops. Thus, it was necessary to deal with vocabulary inferencing strategies. (For full details please refer to Löschmann (1993) and Mühlhaus and Löschmann (1996).) During the workshops, students reported which viewing and vocabulary learning strategies they had employed successfully, and shared with the group their evaluation of these. This open sharing encouraged students to try out new strategies they had previously not thought of, which in turn helped them to take responsibility for and control over their learning. Suggestions which came up were, for example, the use of colours, putting vocabulary in context, building word families, recording vocabulary onto a tape and listening to it. These suggestions could have been made by the tutor, but the fact that they were discovered by the students themselves added to the enjoyment of the course and further enhanced their motivation.

More individual support for students was provided through tutor comments in the journal and during tutor office hours.

CONCLUSION

Through several feedback techniques, such as comments in the journal, questionnaires, individual consultations, and the 'minute paper' (a short evaluation of each workshop) which was described and critically evaluated elsewhere (Mühlhaus 1997), we have established students' views on the aural packages. Many expressed satisfaction about trying out new learning strategies. One cohort of year one students liked the video-based aspect of this programme so much that they asked for more videos in the following semester, a suggestion which we were, naturally, delighted to comply with.

In this context we also regard pre-viewing activities as an important component towards the success of students' work. Chambers (1996) has recently emphasized the importance of pre-listening activities to access students 'knowledge of the language and knowledge of the topic and to arouse certain expectations' (p.25) and curiosity.

It is not easy to develop self-directed and flexible learning and, at the beginning of each year, there are always a few students who are not happy with aural German. They just find tutor-led classes more comfortable. But we seem to have succeeded in convincing students that independent learning is a promising, flexible way of learning. The effectiveness appears to depend highly on the quality of the learning package, on motivation, be it integrative or instrumental, and the instructiveness of the workshop in helping students find their own ways of learning. Tutor comments in student journals and on their performance in the workshops also play a central role in this process.

As we are continuing to improve our packages we are presently focusing on the following areas: to encourage students to exchange their experience, to produce their own learning package, to combine the development of reading and listening comprehension, and to produce adjuncts to the package. Work on a CD-ROM is in progress, which incorporates texts, exercises and tests concerning word formation to increase students' command of receptive vocabulary (Löschmann, forthcoming).

REFERENCES

Chambers, G N (1996) 'Listening? Why? How?' *Language Learning Journal* 14, September pp. 23–7

Löschmann, M (1993) *Effiziente Wortschatzarbeit*, Lang, Frankfurt

Löschmann, M (forthcoming) *CD-ROM: German Word formation* (working title) to be published by Institut für Interkulturelle Kommunikation Ansbach, Jena

Mühlhaus, S (1997) 'Feedback and Motivation', in: Stroinska, M and Löschmann, M (eds) *Motivation and Feedback in Language Teaching and Learning*, Kingston University, Kingston-upon-Thames

Mühlhaus, S and Löschmann, M (1996) 'Learning with the help of strategies for vocabulary and terminology acquisition', in: Gibbs, G (ed) *Improving Student Learning. Using Research to Improve Student Learning*, Oxford Centre for Staff Development, Oxford

Chapter 4

Peer Mentoring through Peer-Assisted Study Sessions

Angus Witherby

The University of New England has one of the largest Schools of Planning in the country. Full-time students number about 50 in each core unit of the four-year undergraduate degree in planning. Most live in halls of residence on campus. This case study describes the application of peer mentoring to the undergraduate teaching of transport planning, a second-year, one semester unit within the programme.

WHAT ARE PEER-ASSISTED STUDY SESSIONS?

Peer-assisted study sessions, (PASS), are a method of providing a flexible, student-driven learning environment through the use of peer-centred communication in voluntary student study groups. Each student study group is facilitated by one or two students from a previous year of the unit. Study groups both tailor their own learning environment within the groups and provide feedback to the wider learning environment thus allowing it to respond flexibly and dynamically to emerging student learning needs. The use of peer-centred communication within the learning groups encourages students to 'take responsibility for their own behaviour and attitudes, to learn how to listen carefully, to think critically and to express themselves accurately....It is a model for empowerment that encourages individuals to reflect more deeply about their own ideas and feelings' (Timpson 1994). This description clearly demonstrates the relevance of the technique to the traditional values espoused for university education. Also of importance is that these skills and competencies overlap substantially with those required for professional practice (Bowie 1996).

WHY APPLY PASS TO TRANSPORT PLANNING?

The unit had been rigidly taught on a traditional lecture/tutorial/practical basis. Greater flexibility was needed to meet a wide variety of student needs and to address a number of problems. The following were the main issues:

- The unit is a compulsory unit which had an historically high failure rate (typically 15–20 per cent).
- The unit was shifting from third year to second year as part of the reorganization of the planning programme. This meant that students were less experienced when attempting the unit.
- Traditional assessment and feedback procedures (for example standard 'end of semester' questionnaires) did not provide any opportunity for modification to be made during the time that the unit was operating. This meant that tailoring to meet the express needs of current students was very difficult.
- There was clear evidence of systematic weakness among a number of students, in basic study skills and orientation towards university level education. This could not be dealt with entirely adequately in the first year.
- The same person covered lectures, tutorials and practical sessions. This meant that a student having a personality clash or other difficulties in relating to the teaching staff did not have any other alternatives.

HOW DOES IMPLEMENTATION WORK?

PASS was initially implemented with the assistance of an experienced trainer in the technique. He undertook the coordination and administration of PASS in consultation with the unit coordinator for the first year. The coordinator then assumed this role as experience was gained.

The unit coordinator selects facilitators for training from previous students who have undertaken the unit and have obtained reasonable grades.

These students are paid a modest hourly sum. In the initial trial only two students were potential candidates and both were used as facilitators. Currently, two of the previous year's facilitators and two new facilitators are being used, each experienced facilitator teaming with a 'novice'. The facilitators are trained by the unit coordinator in a half-day session and meet with the unit coordinator on a weekly basis during semester.

Typically, PASS covers some 75 per cent of the total internal student enrolment in the unit. For a class of 50 students, usually four PASS groups are established, each with ten or eleven students meeting weekly for an hour. The study group sessions are held in the department – although some other units utilize groups based in the halls of residence on campus. Unlike the sessions run in the halls of residence, this programme runs during normal teaching times in gaps between other commitments.

Content of the study group sessions is driven largely by the emerging needs of the students themselves. This creates a customized, flexible learning environment. This flexibility is not only evident week by week, but is also a feature of the individual sessions. In addition to the student driven content, the facilitators also introduce issues from their own experience that the students will find useful.

PERCEIVED BENEFITS OF PASS

The following major benefit areas have been identified after two years of operation.

Teaching programme flexibility

The teaching programme is now driven by student needs. The unit has been restructured so that the primary teaching forum is the student-led tutorial. Lectures, practical and special sessions supplement the tutorials. PASS allows lectures, practical and special sessions to respond dynamically to the emerging needs of the student body as they progress through the unit guided by the tutorials. This ensures that the unit coordinator can vary both content and style as necessary. A disadvantage of this approach is that comparatively short lead times are available for the development and presentation of specialized material. While this is considered a disadvantage, it also has the advantage that the material is fresh and the unit coordinator is less inclined to over-deliver in terms of the quantity of material.

Workload reduction

Although not a major factor in the implementation of PASS in the department, some reduction in workload is apparent. In particular, the availability of PASS has seen the majority of routine enquiries being dealt with by the PASS facilitators. Significantly less time is therefore spent on one-to-one work with students on both problems of basic understanding and study skills, leaving extra time for one-to-one student contact on higher level conceptual matters, and interaction with the PASS facilitators.

Improved tutorial functioning

As indicated above, tutorials are now the major mode of material delivery in the unit. The tutorials are based around a series of 12 questions (one per week) which form the basis of the exam paper. These 12 questions are used as a platform to develop higher cognitive skills in the assemblage and linkage of ideas and concepts in the field of transport planning. The existence of the PASS scheme has enabled rapid and effective skills development within the student body in terms of meeting expectations of a tutorial system of this type. In particular, structural issues involved with the preparation and presentation of papers have been addressed, and recent work is showing enhanced achievement of the desired level of conceptual understanding.

Enhancement of teaching experience

A further benefit of the PASS system has proven to be enhancement of teaching experience. The development of a dynamic and responsive feedback mechanism has resulted in a more pleasurable teaching task as there is a higher degree of certainty that the unit is addressing student needs. This is coupled with a reduction in stress due to the confidence that there are no major structural problems with the unit. An additional area of benefit is the growing dialogue between students and the unit coordinator. This has manifested particularly in tutorials where the unit coordinator and the students are managing genuine advancements in knowledge and understanding beyond that contained within the unit material. This mutual learning and discovery experience assists in maintaining enthusiasm for the unit and is a direct consequence of the enhanced flexibility provided by the technique.

Dealing with key gaps

Another benefit of PASS has been the ability to identify and deal with key gaps in knowledge and/or understanding promptly. A particular example was feedback from PASS concerning processes behind policy development. Although one lecture had been given on policy, students still had difficulties with the topic. A second lecture was presented using case study material which talked about both the theory and practice (i.e. the political reality) of policy development. This precise targeting to student needs and levels of knowledge has been shown to enhance the understanding of key concepts. As a consequence much of the unit material 'falls into place' more readily. The active feedback has significant importance in the annual review of the unit. It can help ensure that key concepts are delivered at an appropriate time and in an appropriate manner in the conduct of the unit.

Other areas of feedback

In addition to unit-specific information, feedback is received on matters such as coordination of assignment loads between units, handling of extensions for assignments, and other areas of departmental policy. PASS is thus proving to be a useful adjunct to the existing formal channels of student representation and feedback on the School of Planning's departmental and course advisory committees.

CONCLUSIONS

PASS has been formally evaluated through student questionnaires, feedback from student facilitators and by discussion with student small groups. PASS has increased student satisfaction with their learning experience and since its introduction the failure rate in the unit has dropped nearly to zero. It is clear that students not attending the PASS sessions also benefit from the change in teaching environment from lecturer-centred expert (although some expert material is still presented) to flexible, student-centred mutual learning. There is also evidence that students are applying the skills and competencies acquired to other courses. Of particular interest is the improvement in academic performance and general confidence of the student facilitators – indeed facilitator positions are now highly sought after. In terms of resources, PASS is resource-neutral in terms of time, and modest in cost at around 500 Australian dollars per semester. It has therefore proved highly cost-effective in enhancing student outcomes.

REFERENCES

Bowie, I J (1996) *What the Market wants from Planning Courses: A Report on the Perceptions of the Planning Industry and of University of New England Planning Graduates*, Department of Geography and Planning, University of New England, Armidale, New South Wales, Australia

Timpson, W M (1994) *Peer Centred Communication for University Students*, The Tertiary Education Institute, University of Queensland, Australia

Chapter 5

Teaching by E-Mail

Chris Smith

This case study describes a psychology and information technology optional half-module which was taught and administered entirely by e-mail to a group of 72 first year, full-time, psychology undergraduates. Although e-mail was adopted because of the lack of available space and the absence of a key member of staff, it offered the additional advantages to students of control over and responsibility for their own learning.

E-MAIL

Electronic mail (e-mail) is used to send and receive messages, but offers many other facilities, two of which were of particular importance for the psychology half-module, namely:

- the 'distribution list' facility, which enables the sender to reach many people with a single message, so that only a few additional key presses were needed to send a message simultaneously to all 72 students;
- the 'attachment' facility allows the user to attach files to a message. Thus a large document could be sent to the students with ease.

E-mail allows a received message to be printed, deleted or retained in a folder for later access. Students had more than enough space in their area on the network to store all the module information.

BACKGROUND TO THE COURSE

Students at the University of Central Lancashire take six modules per year. 'Psychology and Information Technology' is an optional first year half-module, which is taught in the second semester. It follows a compulsory half-module, Information Technology, which teaches basic skills such as use of the University network, wordprocessing and spreadsheets. The information technology module also includes a session on e-mail, including a small and compulsory piece of coursework to demonstrate basic ability to use e-mail.

The psychology module was originally limited to 30 students to allow for the use of one terminal room for one hour per week. However, when an alternative course became unexpectedly unavailable, the module had to accommodate 72 students with no available rooms or staff. E-mail came to the rescue and, as will be outlined below, was a very successful substitute.

THE ORIGINAL VERSION

The module was planned as a course of four lectures and eight hands-on sessions, (see Figure 5.1).

1. **Lecture**: Introduction: the uses of Information Technology (IT) in psychology
2. Methodological applications of IT in psychology*
3. Psychology and the Internet*
4. **Lecture**: Computer-assisted learning
5. Computer-assisted learning*
6. **Lecture**: Artificial intelligence
7. Artificial intelligence (ELIZA)*
8. Machine translation*
9. Expert systems*
10. **Lecture**: Neural networks
11. Neural networks*
12. Human-computer interaction*

*'hands-on' sessions

Figure 5.1 *Psychology and Information Technology syllabus*

The module was to be assessed by the best six or seven short pieces of coursework, which varied from evaluating software (an expert system and a machine translation package, for example) to discussing a general topic via one or two specific studies (methodology and computer-assisted learning, for example). The aim of the course was to focus on those aspects of information technology which are specifically related to psychology. The content of the module thus consisted of a range of topics where psychology and information technology make contact, such as methodology, artificial intelligence, computer-assisted learning and neural networks.

THE E-MAIL VERSION

The content of the e-mail version of the module did not differ from the original version and the differences in teaching method were more apparent than real. These were that:

- no classes took place at timetabled hours;
- there was no face-to-face contact with students;
- all course materials – 'lectures' and details of hands-on sessions, were delivered by e-mail;
- general course details were delivered before the start date for the course; all materials were delivered well before their scheduled use;
- no paper was used for course materials;
- no paper was used for the handing in of coursework (although it was found to be easier to print copies of some coursework in order to be able to return it with written comments on it).

IMPLEMENTATION

A week before the module was due to start all students were e-mailed an outline of the module. This contained the objectives, syllabus and coursework arrangements. Thereafter, students received regular mailings of lecture notes, details of hands-on sessions and of coursework assignments. Although the material could all have been sent at the beginning of the module, some of the facilities for the hands-on sessions were only available for a particular week and it seemed generally sensible to maintain a working schedule and pattern to the course – with deadlines for the submission and return of coursework. Additional contact with students came from a more or less weekly bulletin. This was used to remind students about where the course was at, when the next deadline was, and that they could e-mail the tutor about any matter relevant to the course.

WHAT HAPPENED

Coursework was also delivered to students by e-mail. Of a possible 504 pieces of coursework 417 were actually submitted, with the eight students who failed the course responsible for 32 of the 87 missing pieces of coursework. Thus, most failures resulted from insufficient rather than poor quality coursework. Although the 64 students who passed the course only failed to submit 55 pieces of coursework between them, some of this can probably be accounted for by some students knowing that a mark of 40 per cent was all that was needed to pass the course.

Every student submitted two or more pieces of coursework, indicating that no student lacked the ability to manage the e-mail system. Marks were generally high – with some very high marks for students who submitted six pieces of coursework. No module evaluation questionnaires were used, but solicited feedback produced ten positive and no negative responses.

These findings and the smoothness with which the course ran are taken as a clear demonstration that e-mail can be used successfully as a means of delivering course materials and receiving coursework. For a course which has no absolute requirement for a tutor to be present and which is not based on face-to-face contact, e-mail would seem to be an efficient and effective medium for course delivery.

CONCLUSION

Student performance on and satisfaction with the module were both high. Although the failure rate was rather high, there were no dire consequences of failure and in no case was failure shown to be attributable to the use of e-mail as a teaching medium. It is felt that the module, which was intended to be optional, would not have been chosen by many students, because of its relatively specialist and technological nature. Indeed, it is also felt that the unusual degree of flexibility and support which the use of e-mail offered may have contributed towards a higher success rate and to higher overall marks than would otherwise have been obtained. Delivering material via e-mail is egalitarian: students are no longer dependent on their note-taking abilities and have a full set of course material, which, if printed, they can access at any time.

E-mail is now a standard form of communication in higher education, but, in addition, it may offer distinct advantages as a medium for teaching and learning. While it may lack the richness and completeness of multimedia, this case study shows that e-mail can, for example, be used to:

- distribute written material;
- monitor take-up of that material;
- notify students of timetable arrangements and deadlines;
- submit coursework;
- give feedback.

Conventional lectures thus need not be given, providing that they are largely text-based. Their full content is distributed to all students familiar with e-mail, who then have full freedom to access it and to determine the use they put it to. With the final proviso that e-mail cannot be an adequate substitute for face-to-face contact, it can be stated with confidence that students are not disadvantaged, and benefit in some ways, from the use of this new medium to replace lectures. A more detailed and systematic comparison of different teaching media is now in progress.

Chapter 6

Using a Shell for Delivery and Support for Case-Based Learning in a Networked Environment

Kathy Buckner and Elisabeth Davenport

This case study refers to a networked learning environment developed for a core module in the final (honours) year of an undergraduate degree in Information Management. The module is 'Human Factors in Information Management'. The current cohort comprises 17 full-time students but part-time students can also take the module which is run by the Department of Communication and Information Studies at Queen Margaret College, Edinburgh.

INTRODUCTION

Work on the development of networked learning resources to facilitate flexible and independent learning began during the spring term of 1995. The first version of the module, which involved case-based problem solving in a traditional classroom setting, relied heavily on paper sources. The 1996 version was still largely classroom based, but students were encouraged to interact with a wider range of sources (primarily print), liaise with professionals (by interview and e-mail), and address the design issues which might contribute to the success of a network-based learning package in the Human Factors in Information Management (HFIM) subject area. In 1997 we introduced the HFIM learning environment. This case study reports on the implementation and evaluation of the HFIM learning environment and reflects on the feasibility of utilizing it as a shell for other subject areas – particularly in domains which traditionally have a less technological focus.

IMPLEMENTATION OF THE HFIM LEARNING ENVIRONMENT

A major design focus of the HFIM platform has been the provision, design and representation of spaces for social interaction (eg negotiation, mentoring) when working on case-based learning material. A collaborative, case-based, problem solving approach (Schank 1990, Guzdial *et al.* 1996) has been used to encourage students to interact with the information and learn how to apply theory in practical situations. The HFIM learning environment (described in more detail in Buckner and Davenport 1996; 1997), has been developed using an integrated approach within the World Wide Web (WWW). It comprises five distinct working areas: the query space, the theory base, the case base, the conference space and the diary space. The work areas have been devised to maximize flexibility of access to, and interaction with, the subject domain. The five spaces are as follows:

The diary space directs the students to weekly activities and provides a location for reflection on the learning process.
The query space is used to present problems and issues to the students which would have traditionally been presented in seminar classes. Students use the theory and case bases to assist in the problem solving process.
The theory base is a repository for study notes, references and WWW links to related sites. Students contribute to the theory base by producing extended abstracts of key references.
The case base is an archive of case studies from a range of organizations eg libraries, hospital trusts, multinational companies, and voluntary sector organizations. Students work in groups to create digital documentaries which are then added to the case base.
The conference space enables students to work collaboratively on problems posed within the query space and the case base. Interaction can be undertaken as and when convenient to the student.

EVALUATION OF THE LEARNING ENVIRONMENT IN PRACTICE

Our evaluation focused on three areas:

• The relationship between prior experience and the process of using the environment and associated tools.

- The way in which students use the information presented to them, eg What is the optimum amount of information which should be provided to students? How do students cope with long text items? Do they copy and paste information into their own files? How do they use different media types?

- The effectiveness of this method of course delivery and assessment in relation to student learning, eg Does 'deep' learning occur? Can we measure it? Will students achieve the long-term appropriation of concepts which allow learners to develop a framework for autonomous problem-solving? Can we establish that collaborative preparation of work in the electronic learning environment leads to the benefits that some have predicted? (Silva and Breuleux, 1994).

While questionnaires were used to establish prior knowledge of the content of the HFIM learning environment and the level of expertise and confidence with the WWW, the majority of the issues described above were explored through focus group discussions with students. Student learning was evaluated by examination of the quality of student assessment.

PRELIMINARY EVALUATION RESULTS

Focus group discussions revealed that students had no particular difficulty using the system. One student missed the orientation session due to ill health and reported that she was able to teach herself how to access and use the information in about an hour and a half. The students liked the organization of material into 'spaces' (as described previously) and found the permanent menu a useful navigation aid. Text items in the system are of varying length but this was readily accepted by students, most preferring to print items to use in private study at a later date rather than read them on the screen. Copying and pasting between applications tended not to occur possibly because students working on computers at home do not (as yet) have Internet access. In their course assessment students demonstrated that they were clearly able to integrate and synthesize material from the case base and the theory base.

Our preliminary results of the confidence level of students working with the content of the HFIM learning environment indicate that there has been a clear improvement in student confidence. The feedback at this stage is tentative and based on a small sample.

In our original specification we assumed that a robust and reliable e-mail network would be the main channel of communication. To cover contingencies where this cannot be sustained, we have developed an alternative communication channel using WWW conferencing facilities. Face-to-face contact with the students has been reduced but this has been compensated for by using electronic communication. Students benefit from individual communications with lecturers via e-mail and from collaborative discussions using the conferencing system.

Currently most students access the site from workshops at Queen Margaret College, while a minority of students have WWW access from home and were able to make use of this during their studies. In the coming months we intend to investigate student access from public WWW access points, eg in other academic libraries, cyber cafes, public libraries.

CONCLUSION

The HFIM environment has essentially been a prototype which has enabled us to develop a shell which can be used in the delivery of courses with a non-technological focus. We have built on the experience of students and staff to refine the structure of the shell. The next phase is to examine the ease with which other course materials slot into our 'spaces'. For example, while the theory base, diary space and conference space may be sufficiently generic to use across disciplines, we may find that the case base and query space are not. Content from the teleworking course has already been translated into the shell structure, and in the near future we intend to present materials from a humanities course in this format.

Time and human resources have been the major constraints in the development of this project. Unlike many other networked learning projects, the HFIM learning environment has been developed with very limited funding (£800 from the Scottish Higher Education Funding Council's Strategic Development Initiative and £1000 from an internal grant). A guesstimate of three hours a week of lecturer time over a 30-week period has been needed to develop and manage the system. We hope that what we have achieved with limited resources will encourage others to consider the use of networked environments for learning and teaching.

Acknowledgements

We would like to acknowledge the work undertaken by Adrian Hodge and Alyn Jones (undergraduate students in the Department of Communication and Information Studies) who assisted in the development of the networked learning environments described here.

REFERENCES

Buckner, K and Davenport, E (1996) 'Support issues for case-based learning in an undergraduate human factors class', *Education for Information*, 14(4), pp. 331–42

Buckner, K and Davenport, E (1997) 'Evaluation of a networked learning environment: training and transferability issues', *Proceedings of 2nd British Nordic Conference on Library and Information Studies* (in press)

Guzdial, M; Koldner, J; Hmelo, C; Narayanan, H; Carlson, D; Rappin, N; Hübscher, R; Turns, J and Newstetter, W (1996) 'Computer support for learning through complex problem solving', *Communications of the ACM* 39(4), April pp. 43–5

Schank, R C (1990) 'Case-based teaching: four experiences in educational software design', *Interactive Learning Environments*,1(4) pp. 231–53

Silva, M and Breuleux, A (1994) 'The use of participatory design in the implementation of internet-based collaborative learning activities in K-12 classrooms', *Interpersonal Computing and Technology: an electronic journal for the 21st century*, 2, July, http://quest.arc.nasa.gov/misc/ipct.html#RPD Accessed 02/12/96

Chapter 7

Learning via Multimedia: A Study of the Use of Interactive Multimedia to Teach Chemistry

Chris Smith, Keith Haddon, Edward Smith and Don Bratton

Six lessons in spectroscopy were taught to two groups of second year, full-time chemistry undergraduates. One group followed a programme of traditional lectures. The second group, comprising 25 students, used a multimedia package. The software was specifically designed to foster flexible learning in terms of both when and how it was used, in order not to restrict access and to allow for student-centred approaches to the content. It was intended to encourage active use and student interaction.

MULTIMEDIA

Multimedia can be defined broadly as software which concurrently communicates information through two or more different media such as animation, audio, graphics, images, text and video. Additionally, multimedia is interactive, enabling users to engage with the information in the package and to impose their learning preferences on the software. In practice, most of the media listed above are included, while learner preferences cannot all be accommodated. To date there is also an inadequate understanding of the learning mechanisms which might operate in using multimedia software (Chinien and Hlynka, 1993), nor has existing software been fully evaluated (Gunn, 1994). This case study addresses the evaluation issue in particular.

THE MULTIMEDIA CHEMISTRY PACKAGE

We decided to create a simple, intuitive system with freedom and flexibility for the user, but with sufficient consistency, stability and tools to prevent the user becoming lost or confused. A lesson shell was created from which the series of six lessons on spectroscopy could be produced easily. The shell consisted of basic ways of presenting information and of navigating through the package. It could also be easily used for other material. Spectroscopy was found to be a topic of average difficulty for the students. The shell was not domain-dependent and could, therefore, be readily applied to other, similar subjects.

The software incorporated sound, graphics, text, animation and video into a book metaphor, which enabled the information to be presented as modules, each consisting of an ordered series of multimedia pages, through which the user could progress in any order or direction. Each page contained:

- video and sound of a lecture (this was the same lecture that the control group attended);
- a textual summary;
- a large 'information chunk' containing graphics, video, text, sound or animation or a mixture of these, as appropriate;
- a toolbar giving access to a transcription of the lecture, a glossary, a local map of the lecture and a global map of the course.

IMPLEMENTATION

After a tutorial on the use of the software, the students were left to use the software whenever they wished for as long as they wished, but they were expected to have studied the six lessons by the end of six weeks. The learning environment was quiet and comfortable. To ensure comparability with the lectures in terms of acquired information, the students were told to take notes as they would normally do in a lecture.

Before the course began, all students were given a questionnaire to determine their attitudes towards computers and their experience. Each session was videoed in order to time and plot the students' progress through the software. After each lesson, each student was given a ten-minute test on the material. At the end of the course there was a formal one-hour test and a second attitude questionnaire was given.

RESULTS

As indicated, data was gathered on experience, attitudes, learning methods and student performance on the course – with the following results:

- Experience: all students were familiar with computers, but they had little or no experience with either computer assisted learning or multimedia.

- Attitudes: students expressed positive views both before and after using the package. They liked the availability, structure, reliability and flexibility of the package and particularly liked being in control of their own learning. They saw a future for multimedia in education, but felt it vital to retain some student-teacher interaction.

- Performance: this was measured by course tests and by a 'value-added' score, which was calculated by deducting the spectroscopy course grade from the average grade obtained by the student on other chemistry courses. Compared to the matched control group, who were taught only via lectures, the multimedia students performed neither better nor worse on the course tests. However, a correlation was found between improvement and ability: the lower ability students improved most as measured by the value-added score. No such correlation was found for the control group (see Haddon *et al.*, 1995 for more details).

- Learning methods: although the students adopted individual learning methods and patterns, they were on average more efficient than the control group; ie they took less time to complete a session and covered more material (through repetition and seeking additional information). Their individual learning styles meant that they used the package at different times and for different lengths of time. They repeated different information, used different media and tools within the package and navigated differently. Up to seven distinct infor-mation acquisition and navigation strategies were identified. There was full attendance among the multimedia students, some of whom booked revision sessions.

FLEXIBLE LEARNING?

Although lower ability students might be expected to improve more than higher ability students, because they have more scope for improvement, no such correlation was found for the control group, and the explanation for the matched multimedia group would seem to lie in the teaching method – the multimedia package itself. In particular, it seems likely that the opportunity to control the pace of the learning process favoured the lower ability students. The processes involved in the comprehension and recording of information in lectures may limit what students of lower ability can achieve in lectures, where the pace of the lecture is outside their control. In a multimedia package the information is recorded in advance and students can make notes from it at their own pace. The other features of the multimedia package do not seem to clearly favour students of lower ability.

Whether such advantages show up in performance or not, it was clear from the attitude questionnaires that students identified many features of the multimedia package which enhanced their ability to benefit from their course. These features could roughly be grouped into features about the software itself and features of the empowerment the software offered to the students to manage their own learning.

There is a downside, of course. There were negative comments about the lack of student-teacher contact, which related to the inability of the software to elaborate on information or to answer questions. E-mail contact could perhaps alleviate this. There were also negative comments about the increased reliance on self discipline. Finally, use of multimedia packages currently requires special equipment, special arrangements and special training, although it is likely that the need for these will diminish and eventually disappear.

CONCLUSION

Students' performance is not adversely affected by using multimedia for course delivery. Students' attitudes are generally positive and their learning methods are adjusted to meet their individual requirements. Thus, with reservations, there seems to be considerable scope for multimedia to replace lectures on many courses. The major reservation concerns the resource implications, which currently are considerable – in terms of hardware and software. Establishing a shell does simplify the production of software. Further work is in progress to investigate the links between learning outcomes and learning methods.

REFERENCES

Chinien, C and Hlynka, D (1993) 'Formative evaluation of prototypical products', *Educational Training Technology International* 30:1 pp. 60–5
Gunn, C (1994) *Designing and Evaluating Educational Effectiveness in CBL: Defining the Problem and Designing a Solution*, Institute for Computer-Based Learning, Herriot-Watt University, Edinburgh
Haddon, K A; Smith, C D; Smith, E H and Bratton, D (1995) 'Can learning via multimedia benefit weaker students?' *Active Learning*, 3 pp. 22–7

SECTION II
Flexibility for Work-Based Learners

INTRODUCTION

This section illustrates through case studies, the importance of flexible learning courses for people currently in work. Breen, Hing and Weeks' (Chapter 8) experience of developing a course for the registered club industry in Australia, demonstrates how industry and higher education institutions can work together to produce a course that meets the needs of the student (that is the employee) and the employer. There has been a growth in the number of academic courses for non-traditional students which has been fuelled by the requirement of continuing professional development to meet the needs of professionals and their statutory/regulatory bodies. Grundy, Lawton and Taylor (Chapter 9) review the distance learning course they created for nurses, where reflection on professional practice and the learning experience is also encouraged. McArdle and McGowan (Chapter 10) also endorse this approach through the development of personal portfolios (the use of portfolios is also explored further in Chapter 17; Ure). Their course also consulted with employers to identify their specific requirements.

Askham (Chapter 11) was concerned about the declining numbers on a course in estates and property management; the institution invited past and present course members to identify how the programme might be improved. The need for greater flexibility was identified; the course was adapted and changed to fit the needs of all stakeholders including: students, staff and institutions. Oldroyd (Chapter 12) also endorses empowerment by users of higher education; the course, developed initially at Bristol, utilizes the student's knowledge and skills and draws on Schön's work on reflection. As with other case studies, greater flexibility has meant that this course is also run in other countries. Garner and Longman's (Chapter 13) example is a masters programme for those involved in teaching individuals with special educational needs. They developed two distance learning modules to meet the needs of a student who moved away from the geographical area and so they are now able to offer parts of the course either on campus or at a distance. Shipway (Chapter 14) discusses the changes in nurse education (also discussed by Grundy *et al.* in Chapter 9) and the need for greater flexibility to meet the requirements of this large and diverse group of students. Finally, McCormack (Chapter 15) considers the development of a postgraduate modular course in the development of flexible learning. The case study reinforces the importance of linking theory with practice.

Chapter 8

Flexible Learning for Australian Club Managers

Helen Breen, Nerilee Hing and Paul Weeks

This case focuses on the Bachelor of Business in Club Management, a six-year, part-time course developed by the School of Tourism and Hospitality Management, Southern Cross University in Lismore, Australia, in conjunction with the Club Managers' Association of Australia. The course has been offered since 1993, and currently has about 130 students enrolled in 24 subject units. The course is offered by distance education only, with employment in the registered club industry a prerequisite for entry. The desire and demand for more professional standards and management expertise in tourism and hospitality industries has been the common impetus for developing courses, such as this one, tailored to the specific needs of the club industry.

INTRODUCTION

Currently, there are around 5600 registered clubs in Australia, with around 6.9 million members (Ross, 1996, p.1). Their core activities are poker machine gaming, provision of food and beverage, entertainment and various types of sports facilities. Career progression in the industry has traditionally been time serving or 'up through the ranks'. However, numerous factors have led to the demand for more educated managers. These include an increasingly competitive environment for club gambling products, the legislation of gaming machines in clubs in most Australian jurisdictions, greater numbers of customers and employees to manage, higher turnover, complex legal, security and financial obligations associated with machine gaming, and stringent controls over club assets. The increased scale of most clubs, and the greater diversity of product mix have placed unprecedented demands on club managers to maintain competitive advantage. Thus a 'good organizer' or 'top sports person' is no longer considered sufficient for managing modern day clubs.

The aim of this case study is to document student access, support and responsibilities in the Bachelor of Business in Club Management, as it attempts to effectively meet the needs of the registered clubs industry. Access, or removing barriers to learning, involves incorporating educational achievements within industrial awards, industry selection of students, flexible time frames for course delivery, multiple entry and exit points, recognition of prior learning, articulation and credit transfer. Support appropriate to individual learners' needs can be seen as flexible delivery modes; tutorial support, appropriate study materials and effective communication systems. Responsibility is seen as students taking control of their own learning and includes workshop and/or assessment strategies.

STUDENT ACCESS

The course structure and sequence of units are predicated upon the levels, competencies and career paths developed in the Club Managers industrial award.

Most students are employed in the club industry at management level. As employers pay the course fees, they are integral in helping to select students who have competencies appropriate for managerial positions in the industry and the capacity to successfully complete the programme. Thus the programme is open to all club personnel working in the industry and sponsored by their club.

A key feature of the programme is its suitability for people holding demanding positions and not necessarily able to participate in formal courses conducted at set times and locations. Course flexibility (study load, time extensions, tutor decisions on individual cases) assists their motivation to complete the study programme, rather than withdraw or fail due to work commitments. Study units commence twice yearly, with most students studying two units each semester, although those under heavy work pressure are likely to study only one. Students can exit from any level of the course. To obtain an award they must have successfully completed the compulsory units that comprise that particular award.

Students may apply for recognition of prior learning based on work-place competencies, assessed by a research task or written examination. Alternatively, recognition of prior learning can be granted on the basis of appropriate previous studies. Articulation and credit transfer arrangements have been negotiated with other educational organisations such as technical and further education colleges (TAFE), the Club Managers Development Association, and workplace assessment programmes. These arrangements help eliminate transition problems associated with gaps between courses, and among students who were expecting to attain club education awards through previous Australian Qualifications Framework accreditation.

STUDENT SUPPORT

Tutors for each unit are selected on the basis of industry experience, academic qualifications and teaching experience, particularly in distance education. Quality and consistency are assured by programme policies regarding student contact, assignments, feedback, marking, teletutorials, phone calls, assignment extensions, assistance for marginal students and tutors' meetings.

Study materials for each unit draw on input from both academic and industry specialists and include an introductory guide, study guide and book of readings. Extra materials such as resource books, text books, video and audio tapes are also provided. Student learning is enhanced through practical learning activities, set readings, wider reading, field observations, assessable written assignments and research. An academic review of course material takes place every year, while a review of one level of the programme is conducted every four years by external club industry reviewers. Thus far, industry reviewers have been very positive about the content, relevance and depth of course material.

Students can participate in three teleconference tutorials per semester, organized by tutors and funded by the university. Audio tapes record teletutorials for those unable to participate, generally about 33 per cent of students.

Because most students are mature, with little formal education, two video tapes were produced to assist study and communication skills. These aim to enhance students' understanding of academic expectations, clarify academic essay and report writing, and develop reading and note-taking skills. The videos were designed to be active learning tools and are accompanied by several pages of notes. Students keep the videos and use them frequently, especially when writing assignments or reviewing a graded assignment. Students have consistently evaluated the videos as 'excellent' learning tools.

Three newsletters each semester keep students informed and help reduce feelings of isolation, common amongst distance education students. Newsletters report on recent happenings in the course and the university, topics for teletutorial discussions, pre-test applications, evaluation forms, library information, tutor profiles and general learning assistance.

STUDENT RESPONSIBILITY

All students are employed full-time in demanding and responsible positions. To recognize the students' work circumstances, most units require three written assessment items, spaced evenly throughout the semester. Most assessment items are theory based, but reflect practical work experience in a club environment through case studies or responses to club problems.

Work rosters in clubs usually require managers to work long, sometimes unexpected hours, resulting in unpredictable attendance at subject workshops. Three-day residential schools are held at the university campus in Lismore each semester, and workshops are often held at industry conferences and trade shows.

The typical student in the programme is likely to be male, between 26 and 45 years, and in a full-time senior management position in a New South Wales (NSW) club. Most have a TAFE qualification or in some cases hold a previous university degree. Approximately 80 per cent are male and 20 per cent female. The current student profile, their relatively young age and increasing numbers in the course, reflect changing professional and educational expectations in the club industry. The certificate is increasingly seen as the basic educational criteria essential for club positions. Encouragingly, Sims (1996) found that there had been a shift in the proportion of managers holding a diploma or degree qualification since the skills audit in the Futuretech Report (1991). It could be expected that as younger, qualified, but possibly less experienced managers progress in their careers, the basic educational criteria will gradually move towards the degree qualification.

CONCLUSION

Three years after the launch of the Bachelor of Business in Club Management, 321 students in the course have completed over 1000 units, with most having completed the Certificate level. The university's experience with the Bachelor of Business in Club Management has found that industry-specific education at a tertiary level is not only important, but can be a precipitating factor in the development and maintenance of workplace change. Changing workplace practices is essential to overall change management in organizations such as registered clubs, which operate in a dynamic environment. Recent course evaluation has been positive, but the challenge is to continue to ensure that the programme remains industry-relevant in the future while maintaining academic rigor.

REFERENCES

Futuretech Pty Ltd (1991) *Final Report of the Skills Audit, Training Needs Analysis and New Award Study of Managers in the Registered Clubs Industry*, Registered Clubs Association of New South Wales, Sydney

Ross, M (1996) 'President's Column', *Club News*, Licensed Clubs Association of Victoria Inc., April, p. 1

Sims, W J (1996) 'A Comparison of Recruitment and Renumeration Practices in the Licensed Club Industries of NSW and Queensland', Paper presented at the *Australian Tourism and Hospitality Research Conference*, Coffs Harbour, Australia, February

Chapter 9

Distance Learning in Post-Registration Nurse Education

Maggie Grundy, Sally Lawton and Armida Taylor

This is a distance-learning degree course for post-registration nurses provided by the Associate Faculty of Nursing, Midwifery and Community Studies of the Robert Gordon University, Aberdeen.

INTRODUCTION

The Bachelor in Nursing/Bachelor in Community Health Nursing was developed in 1992 in response to student demand for a flexible course which would provide registered nurses with the opportunity to develop their professional knowledge and competence, and to gain academic accreditation at degree level. It also offered nurses, who had gained recordable qualifications at certificate or diploma level, the opportunity to enter an educational programme with accreditation for their prior learning.

The course was developed in accordance with contemporary trends in nurse education where, in keeping with the principles of adult learning, a student-centred approach underpinned the curriculum development. Furthermore, the course was designed to be delivered on a distance learning basis accompanied by core residential weeks for each module. Students were encouraged to undertake the six modules of part one of the course at their own pace, in the order of their choice and then to plan an individual programme of study for part two. This enabled students to complete their studies in accordance with the University regulations while fulfilling their personal, domestic and professional obligations. The team have developed an administrative system that copes with this flexibility. A member of the course team is dedicated to the complex administration of the course recording student progress. Figure 9.1 shows the structure of this course.

<table>
<tr><td colspan="2" align="center">**Part One**</td><td align="center">**Part Two**</td></tr>
<tr><td>Professional issues</td><td>Health promotion</td><td>Analysis of practice</td></tr>
<tr><td>Behavioural science</td><td>Communication and teaching</td><td>Current issues in health</td></tr>
<tr><td>Management</td><td>Epidemiology and research</td><td>Research-based nursing practice</td></tr>
</table>

Figure 9.1 *Structure of the BA in Nursing/BA in Community Health Nursing course*

In 1991, the United Kingdom Central Council (UKCC) produced the 'Post Registration Education and Preparation for Practice' consultative document which proposed that reflection-on-practice should be used as a means of providing evidence that action had been taken to develop professional knowledge and competence (this became a requirement in 1995). Analysis of practice was, therefore, a core element of the curriculum in part two of the course encouraging the development of reflective practice.

Moreover, the innovatory design of the course afforded the University the opportunity to offer further degree programmes in a variety of specialisms. One of these was the cancer nursing route which was added to the existing structure in 1995 as a response to the demand for cancer nursing education.

THE CANCER NURSING ROUTE

Two options were written for this route. The first was designed to comply with the UKCC requirements for specialist practice and necessitated a combination of 50 per cent theory and 50 per cent practice. The second was a theoretical route which reflected the existing structure of the BA in Nursing course.

The three theoretical units in the specialist practice route were devised to reflect both the specialist cancer nursing content and UKCC requirements, including 16 weeks clinical practice. Following discussion with the National Board for Nursing, Midwifery and Health Visiting for Scotland, it was agreed that a specialist practitioner in cancer nursing should be familiar with patient care at all stages of the disease process, and with nursing care of individuals undergoing all treatment modalities.

This required students to undertake clinical practice where individuals were receiving chemotherapy, radiotherapy, surgery and palliative care. The majority of students would therefore have to have some time out from their own area of practice to fulfil the course requirements. In order to maintain the flexible philosophy of the BA in Nursing, the length and timing of each placement is negotiated with individual students and is dependent on previous experience, work commitments and availability of clinical experience and supervision within clinical areas.

STUDENT SUPPORT

The course team is very aware of the need for organized student support within this distance learning course (Lawton, 1996). For many of the students, a considerable length of time has passed since they received any formal education. In addition, they often have preconceived ideas about the nature of higher education and their own ability to succeed. When their concerns about this are compounded by distance learning as a unfamiliar mode of education, the need for support is paramount.

Every student is allocated a personal tutor whom they meet during each of the core residential weeks. During the self-study phase of the course, the student can phone, fax or e-mail the tutor if and when any guidance is required. This enables an effective student-tutor relationship to develop over time and provides 'continuity of care' for the student. If the relationship does not work out, then the student can move to another tutor.

One of the roles of the tutor is to establish the particular support needs of each student and help the student plan their learning development during the course. Previous learning experiences can be discussed and any concerns identified. One of the major anxieties that students experience is a lack of confidence in their writing skills. As the mode of assessment is continuous, these are important skills to develop. Within each modular core week, sessions on essay writing and other study skills are offered. Anxiety usually begins to lessen once the first essay has been submitted, marked and returned to the student. If a student fails any essay, but particularly the first one, the tutor will discuss the reasons why with the student as well as spend time re-building the lost confidence. The team invests considerable time in writing feedback for student essays.

The individualized support for the student continues throughout the course. The tutor can help the student to network with other people in their geographical area (with consent from all parties). This contact with other students is also an important form of support for students and counters the feeling of isolation that can occur in distance learning. Once the course is completed, the final phase of support is concerned with reviewing the student's progress and helping them to realize their achievements.

ADVANTAGES AND DISADVANTAGES OF THE PROGRAMME

The annual course appraisal system has allowed the students to highlight the advantages and disadvantages of the course. The advantage of offering this type of programme is the ability to study without having to leave work or attend regular classes each week. This flexibility means that students can alter their programmes of study to suit their own circumstances. The provision of support for the students adds to the quality of their educational experience. In the options that require a period of clinical practice, the placements are negotiated on a flexible basis with clinically based colleagues who undertake the supervision of students on behalf of the university.

The benefit of having the core residential weeks ensures that the students meet their tutor and other students, as well as providing them with a break from their usual routine. It also gives them access to the library facilities in the University.

These advantages are reflected in the low drop-out rate which has remained below 10 per cent since its original development in 1992. This is a low attrition rate in comparison to other distance learning programmes where over 50 per cent of enrolled students did not complete their studies prior to the introduction of proactive student support (Zajkowski, 1993).

However, there are disadvantages in terms of course planning and development costs as well as the workload involved in providing individualized student support. For the self-funding student the fees are expensive, and within the University a lack of understanding abounds about the development time and costs in contrast to more traditional forms of education. It is frequently perceived that distance learning is a 'cheap option'. Our experience and other evidence would refute this. In planning and developing a distance learning course, sound business planning is required to determine that the investment costs of producing a distance-learning course can be met by student uptake. In the example of the cancer nursing route, it took approximately one year to produce the materials needed for the students. In addition, the course team are relatively unique in writing, administering and supporting students on the same course.

The course team are also aware of the need for students to be able to access library facilities. With the development of new technology, it is anticipated that information will be available online for students in the future. This has long-term implications for alternative modes of flexible course delivery.

CONCLUSION

The Bachelor in Nursing/Bachelor in Community Health Nursing was in the forefront of post-registration continuing education, by providing a flexible educational experience at degree level for registered nurses. It has also provided them with the opportunity to reflect-on-practice, in order to provide evidence of professional development. This opportunity for the students, however, has also been countered by the costs of development for the institution.

REFERENCES

Lawton, S (1996) *The Effectiveness of Educating Community Nurses by Distance Learning*, Unpublished PhD Thesis, The Robert Gordon University, Aberdeen

United Kingdom Central Council (1991) *Post Registration and Practice and Project Report*, UKCC, London

Zajkowski, M (1993) 'Business students learning at a distance: one form of pre-enrolment counselling and its effect on retention', *Distance Education* 14 (2) pp. 331–53

Chapter 10

Professional Development through Reflective Inquiry

Karen McArdle and Ian McGowan

A Bachelor degree (BA) in Professional Development was designed to meet the needs of mid-career professionals in the social professions wanting to develop from diplomates to graduates. The degree is a distance learning, modular programme; it aims to develop the students both academically and by enabling them to become more effective in practice.

INTRODUCTION

Until the introduction of the BA in Professional Development in 1993, there was a dearth of opportunities in Scotland and further afield for mid-career professionals in the social professions, such as community education and social work, to engage in continuing professional development activities particularly with respect to award-bearing study. In many of the social professions served by Northern College, initial training had been to diploma level, eg two year diploma in social work or community education and, in the early 1990s, many of these courses of initial training were moving towards three-year degree programmes. This created a demand from existing diplomates for opportunities to continue their study to degree level. For these reasons, and because of the interest in the Department of Community and Continuing Education to explore the development of an appropriate pedagogy to meet the needs of mid-career professionals, the BA was planned as a final year degree programme for diplomates whose prior learning could be accredited for entry into a final year undergraduate degree.

THE FLEXIBLE LEARNING APPROACH

The Department of Community and Continuing Education worked closely with employers to identify mid-career needs, particularly those of a generic nature. The outcome of our consultations was a distance learning modular programme with 'more effective practice' emerging as the principal aim. The distance learning modular structure was justified by the geographical location of Northern College in the north of Scotland, and the commitment of the institution to provide equality of opportunity for those living in rural and remote areas. The 'more effective practice' theme marked a paradigm shift in our thinking away from a traditional 'content' design, and a pedagogy rooted in a conception of learning as the transmission and application of existing knowledge.

'My bedrock assumption is that many of the shortcomings of continuing education are due to inappropriate choices about the ends to which the minds of professions should be cultivated. Specifically most continuing education has followed a model set at pre-service level in focusing on the transmission of formal abstract knowledge' (Cevero, 1992,p.92).

In our course design, we recognized a clear need to engage participants from the outset in processes which enabled them to use their prior and concurrent experiences together with their studies in order to reconstruct professional knowledge and practices. Since it could be assumed that course participants would be more familiar with the idea of transmission than construction and re-construction of knowledge, there were clear implications for the course design, requiring explicit sharing of the distinctive philosophy which was to underpin the course and the nature of learning support.

REFLECTIVE INQUIRY AS A KEY LEARNING PROCESS IN CONTINUING PROFESSIONAL DEVELOPMENT

During the 1980s and early 1990s, largely as a result of the writing of Schön (1983, 1987), the notion of the reflective practitioner has gained currency in courses of professional development in Britain, particularly in the field of education. There has also been a growing though modest interest in experiential learning. If course participants were to be in a position to reconstruct their professional practice they needed not only 'to learn about' reflective practice, experiential learning and inquiry methods, but these processes needed to become embedded in their practice. It was decided to include three modules, from the total of eight which diplomates are required to complete for the degree as core studies. These core studies included the philosophy of professional practice (including reconstruction of professional knowledge) and reflective inquiry (including reflective practice and research methods). In terms of flexibility, the significance of the emphasis on reflective inquiry as a generic process opened up the course to a range of professions beyond the initial target group.

STRUCTURE AND CONTENT

Consultation with employers had identified that, at mid-career, middle management issues were a priority to be addressed in course content. Generic management modules together with some more specialist modules for targeted situations were developed to form an optional range. Finally, if course participants were to put their learning together holistically, it was considered appropriate to include a two module equivalent integrative professional project as the final component. The structure which emerged is illustrated in Figure 10.1.

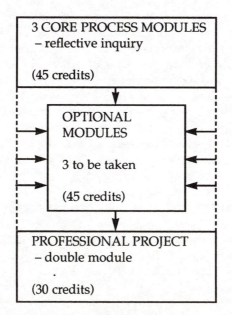

Figure 10.1 *BA in Professional Development course structure*

OPEN LEARNING

While many traditional open/distance learning courses have been 'open' in the sense that they reduce the barriers of distance, they have been 'closed' in terms of prescribing content and assessment. This course has sought to embrace openness not only as a practice but also as a philosophy and, consequently, an action learning approach has been adopted in the distance learning materials (Rowntree, 1994). This has sought to engage participants in an interactive way with their practice through tasks and activities, and encourages participants to take ownership of their learning. This is reinforced by the adoption of an informal writing style in the distance learning materials, encouraging participants to locate their learning in their own professional context and their opportunities for negotiated assessment.

MAKING THE CONNECTIONS: LEARNER SUPPORT

In achieving a flexible design in which the processes of the course are highly emphasized, it has been necessary to put in place design features which encourage and enable participants to find their own appropriate route. Two pivotal features are the use of personal portfolios and the construction of the personal support structure. We have encouraged participants to make on-going use of a personal portfolio to make the connections they themselves see between elements of their practice and the content of the course. The connections can be made in either direction. For example, in some cases participants' reading connects with prior or concurrent experiences. On other occasions their practical knowledge, ie what they encounter in practice, connects with their previous reading in the course content. The personal portfolio maximizes the connections between course content and the work context, and provides an external memory to which participants can return for systematic reflection. Figure 10.2 illustrates the way in which process, content and context are interpreted.

In addition to establishing means to support reflection, we were conscious of the need that reflective practitioners studying at a distance would have active, planned and skilled challenge and support. This would enable them to move from self reflection to a kind of practical theorizing and constant justification of their actions, and to move personal knowing to a more public form of knowing. The content of the first module on the course, 'Professional development', assists participants to explore issues of challenge and support and, as part of the assessment, to produce a design and a justification for their individual support network.

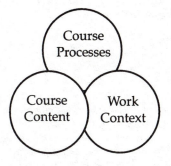

Figure 10.2 *Integration of process, content and context*

The kinds of network which have been in use have varied enormously depending on a range of factors including geographical location, the availability of people to meet within a face-to-face situation, and the availability of appropriate technologies. Participants have been encouraged to think of the network not so much as experts but very much as people whom Lieberman (1989) refers to as 'defining their success not by becoming another group of specialists, but rather by engaging in the building of a culture of inquiry and improved learning environment' (cited in Day, 1993, p.88). In practice, the support networks which have been established are a combination of 'vertical' support through, for example, line managers, and also 'horizontal' support systems, such as peer groups.

CONCLUSION

The planning of the BA in Professional Development has provided an opportunity to develop a course which placed an emphasis on course processes rather than a predominantly content focus. The process orientation has enabled the course to achieve a high level of flexibility in terms of the target audience, and the range of issues which practitioners have been able to bring on to the learning agenda while studying at a distance. Allowing participants to explore issues of challenge and support, results in a highly individual support network. Central to the success of the course have been the sharing of the philosophy of the course at the outset, the high quality of the interactive distance learning materials, and the support given to participants to learn how to engage in reflective inquiry.

Our experience of designing and operating and our evaluations of the BA in Professional Development have now led to the extension of the course into a three year BA scheme, and the development of a Masters degree in Advanced Professional Studies.

REFERENCES

Cevero, R (1992) 'Professional Practice, Learning & Continuing Education' *International Journal of Lifelong Education* 11 (2) pp. 91–101

Day, C (1993) 'Reflection: A Necessary But Not Sufficient Condition for Professional Development' *British Educational Research Journal* 19 (1) p. 88

Rowntree, D (1994) *Exploring Open and Distance Learning*, Kogan Page, London

Schön, D A (1983) *The Reflective Practitioner*, Basic Books, New York

Schön, D A (1987) *Educating the Reflective Practitioner*, Jossey Bass Inc., San Francisco

Chapter 11

Workplace Learning: Removing the Barriers

Phil Askham

This case study considers the review of a work-based learning programme leading to a certificate in estates and property management which was experiencing low levels of participation, and where the course team felt it was important to examine the barriers to participation on the programme by means of direct contact with students and prospective students, in order to tap into their perceptions. It describes how a flexible evaluation strategy was used to identify these barriers and shows how this information was used to inform the review process.

INTRODUCTION

The review of the certificates in estates and property management which took place in 1996 coincided with a much wider review of all training and accreditation being undertaken by the employer, the Employment Service Estates Branch. While the scheme had proved to be successful, with large numbers of staff enrolled and a consistently high standard of work submitted for assessment, the number of staff actively participating had started to decline and with few completing the awards.

To inform the review of the programme, three workshops were held during November 1995 at the hotel which the employer normally uses for its residential training courses. In all, 22 staff attended in groups of nine, seven, and six. The participants were representative of a good cross-section of the 63 staff enrolled.

THE REVIEW PROCESS

Our evaluation was placed towards the naturalistic end of the continuum identified by Bothams (1986), exploring a number of issues without preconceived hypotheses and starting with student perceptions. It also reflected the action approach identified by Aspinwall *et al.* (1992, p.3): 'The greatest need for those engaged in action is for formative evaluation: reliable information about the strengths, weaknesses, advantages and disadvantages of a particular nature or development which enables the most effective next step to be identified.' The method was flexible enough to allow unanticipated participants' issues to emerge and for information gathered to feed directly into decision making about the future of the programme.

The workshop methodology was based on a series of structured group sessions, originally devised by Drew and Payne (1993), developed for the national Unit for the Development of Adult Continuing Education (UDACE) project on learning outcomes, where it was used to gather student perceptions by the participating institutions (Otter, 1992). It had as its starting point descriptions of two other strategies, nominal group technique (Boud, 1986) and a method of gathering student perceptions as used at Wirral Metropolitan College (Wirral Metropolitan College, 1990).

The methodology is described in detail by Askham, Challis and Drew (1997, in progress) but consists of small and large group discussion using a series of questions. The specific questions actually used were wide ranging:

- What are the barriers to participating in the initiative?
- What possible solutions are there to these barriers?
- What are the major elements of your job?
- What skills do you need in carrying out your job?
- What knowledge do you need in carrying out your job?
- What aspects of assessment on the scheme do you like and which do you dislike?
- What support do you need to succeed on the scheme?
- What ideas do you have for changing the structure of the scheme?

In broad terms the workshops aimed to identify the barriers to participation and give participants the opportunity to address them and to influence the revision of the programme.

THE BARRIERS

Gibbs (1992) suggests that effective participative learning facilitated by work-based learning must be desired by the student, within their capabilities, and feasible in the work environment. These conditions are echoed in the barriers identified in the workshops which are summarized in Figure 11.1.

Support	• Participants needed more direction on how to work through the awards
	• They needed more support from the University and the employer
Clarity	• The documentation for the awards lacked clarity, often bound up in educational jargon and difficult language
	• The learning outcomes were difficult to understand
	• There was both too much and too little information leading to both confusion and a lack of clear direction
Motivation	• What are the values of the awards both within and outside the workplace?
	• Would they enhance employment prospects?
Time pressures	• Staff are under increasing pressure within the work place
Morale	• Threats to job security and permanence
Relevance	• Some learning outcomes seemed irrelevant within a rapidly changing and varied job role
	• There was a need for more flexibility
Confidence	• The return to structured learning was daunting

Figure 11.1 *Barriers to entry and participation*

It was clear that these barriers needed to be addressed by the Univer-sity and by the employer. Clearly, many could not be resolved by the University (time and money for example), but the others (lack of information and guidance) could and might indeed help to alleviate some of the apparently more intractable problems. In particular, the University needed to provide better support, increase flexibility, offer a clearer framework for personal development, action planning, induction and study skills development.

DISCUSSION

We believe that the sessions generated far more detailed and valid information than would have been possible by questionnaire. A high level of agreement emerged on the need for support. Participants stressed the need for a commitment from the employer to provide in-house support for learners and study leave, or at least time allocations for work on assignments. There was a consensus on the need for regular contact with university tutors and with other learners, for more written guidance, and for rapid and supportive feedback.

It was evident that a range of job functions were common to all participants, but that there were variations which needed to be accommodated by greater flexibility in the learning outcomes. A general functional drift away from specialism towards the more generic role of consultant management demanded awards which focused more clearly on this management role.

On assessment, the need for the imposition of deadlines, more effective feedback and guidance was expressed. There was a wide diversity of views on the most appropriate forms of assessment, which again seemed to identify the need for greater flexibility and choice in the mode of assessment.

Participants suggested a range of practical ideas which were incorporated into the awards. A great deal was revealed about their perceptions of the organization. It seemed we were tapping into feelings, identifying suspicions and generally eliciting a much deeper level of response than was anticipated.

Each review workshop concluded with a genuine and mutual sense of collaboration, with the facilitators feeling they had learned some important general lessons about the nature of the staff–student relationship. It was very important, for example, that the participants were able to develop a sense of ownership in the course and the workshops themselves helped to foster this. The participants clearly enjoyed the experience and actually learnt a lot more about the course. What was particularly gratifying was the comment that the workshops had been a positive developmental experience with the sessions providing helpful clarification of their own perceptions.

The final outcome of the review process, of which the workshops were only a part, was to produce an award framework which addressed many of the concerns of the participants. In particular the revised awards have provided:

- a clearer definition of the initiative's aims and objectives which were widened to emphasize personal development;
- indicative learning outcomes written in more relevant and transparent terms incorporating forms of words generated by the students;
- greater flexibility in indicative learning outcomes and assessment modes which give room for choice and negotiation;
- development of a workable support strategy, including specific ideas from the students;
- the development of course administration processes which involve the participants;
- a more streamlined and flexible assessment strategy;
- a re-focusing of ownership of the initiative away from the university and the employer in favour of the participants.

CONCLUSION

The review workshops provided a deep insight into all aspects of the provision from the student perspective and fostered a genuine spirit of cooperation between the course team and the students. This enabled the course team to proceed in the planning process with greater confidence. At the same time the participants came to new realizations which seemed to generate greater motivation and a sense of ownership.

REFERENCES

Askham, P; Challis, M and Drew, S (1997, in progress) *Evaluation/Course Review: Gathering Student Perceptions by Structured Group Sessions*

Aspinwall, K; Simpkins, T; Wilkinson, J F and Macauley, N J (1992) *Managing Evaluation in Education. A Developmental Approach*, Routledge, London

Bothams, J (1986) 'Throwing Light on Evaluation?' *Management Education and Development* 17 (1) Spring, pp. 65–73

Boud, D (1986) *Implementing Student Self-Assessment*, Higher Education Research and Development Society of Australia, Australia

Drew, S and Payne, R (1993) 'Student Perceptions of their Personal Development through Higher Education and their Preparedness for Employment' in: Eggins, H (ed) *Arts Graduates: their Skills and their Employment*, Falmer Press, London

Gibbs, G (1992) *Improving the Quality of Student Learning*, Technical and Educational Services Ltd, Bristol

Otter, S (1992) *Learning Outcomes in Higher Education*, Unit for the Development of Adult Continuing Education (UDACE), London

Wirral Metropolitan College/Training Agency (1990) *Learning Gain in Further Education and Achievement Based Resourcing Project, Bulletin 2*, Wirral Metropolitan College

Chapter 12

Empowering School Managers through Flexible Learning

David Oldroyd

The case study portrays a shift of higher education on-site to the school, requiring a new role for the providers of external support. The locus of control of and responsibility for learning shifts to the teachers themselves, thereby empowering their choice and their action. One spin-off has been the transfer of the methodology to Poland where 7000 school managers are now using several of the units.

INTRODUCTION

'Empowerment' is truly a management buzz word of the 1990s. Its meaning is even more slippery than the meaning of 'flexible learning', but there is wide acceptance that both empowerment and flexible learning are 'good things'. Both of these concepts provide themes for this case study of an innovation in higher education provision for school managers. They feature in the quest to integrate the management development of individual school managers with the process of school improvement. In 1989 the School of Education at the University of Bristol received a grant from the University Grants Committee (now the Higher Education Funding Council for England) for curriculum innovation in higher education.

We used the development time and funding to devise a print-based flexible learning package which would meet the management needs of teachers who had responsibilities for managing other adults in their schools. The key target groups were middle managers, heads of faculties and departments, and pastoral team leaders and coordinators, many of whom had had little opportunity for sustained, structured and supported management development. Our aim was to provide flexibility of access by designing a course which could be pursued at home and in the workplace, at the students' own pace, giving students a wide degree of choice of the topics for detailed study, particularly in the design of an action research project. The project serves two purposes: first, to improve individual managerial performance (in addition to understanding); and second, to contribute to the development of the school. The 3000-word action research project became the assignment which was submitted for evaluation. It brings together the results of self and school improvement efforts with the acquisition of academic qualifications. Each assignment earns the teacher 10 credit points towards a nested sequence of awards: Certificate 40 credit points; Diploma 80 credit points; M.Ed 120 credit points.

RATIONALE

In its influential report 'The Way Forward' (Department of Education and Science, 1990) the School Management Task Force (SMTF) advocated a fundamental shift of emphasis in professional learning towards self-directed but supported study in the workplace, focusing on performance in addition to the acquisition of knowledge and with an agenda determined by the school. The thinking behind this was influenced by theories such as those of Kolb (1984) and Schön (1983) relating to experiential learning and reflective practice. These theories broadened the definition of professional learning, recognising that conventional training removed from everyday realities often had an 'otherworldliness' which failed to connect with the realities of everyday working life. The shift of emphasis advocated by the SMTF saw the teacher and the school manager as problem solvers and knowledge creators, rather than learners dependent on the expertise of the outside trainer. The adoption of a flexible learning approach to management development within the context of a higher educational accredited programme was entirely in line with the national strategic lead given by the SMTF at the beginning of the decade.

THE MANAGEMENT SELF-DEVELOPMENT PROGRAMME

Our challenge was to integrate conventional study of educational management with the development of professional performance and school improvement. Figure 12.1 summarizes the components of the programme.

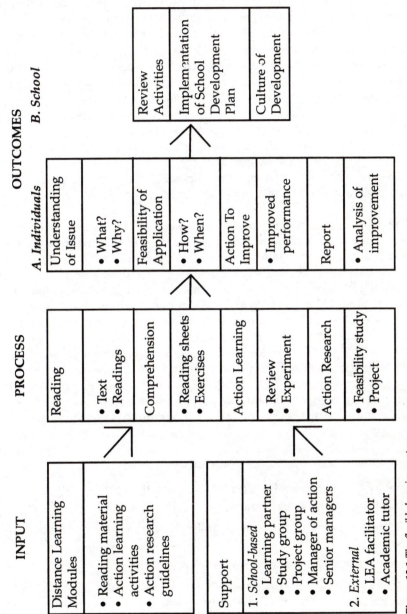

Figure 12.1 *The flexible learning system*

The learner works from the issue (a few pages of authored text sometimes augmented by a selected, copyright-released reading) to the activity (which invites application of the issue to the learner's own situation and performance and leads to the question of whether action for improvement is feasible). This sequence culminates in the framing of an action plan for such an intervention in one's own situation. For students registered for the accredited programme, this is the first point of contact with the external tutor who assists in the design of the project and, on its completion, assesses the report which comprises the formal assignment. Frequently there is 'managed action' in the school, when a professional tutor or member of senior staff negotiates and supports the project on behalf of the school. For example, these assignments can report and analyse the implementation of aspects of the school development plan for the student's own department, or conduct a systematic review which contributes to the planning process.

The content of the core programme is structured around three packages made up of a study and assignment guide, a book containing the text and readings, and a book containing the activities for linking the issues to the learner's own situation and performance. The packages seen as a whole try to integrate personal, professional and organizational development, and are entitled: 'Managing Myself', 'Managing My Team', 'Managing the School'. One ten-credit assignment is produced for each package. In addition to the core units, a number of specialized units have been designed. They include a unit on the methodology of action research to assist students in the production of their projects ('Action Research for School Managers') and units on 'Managing Special Educational Needs', 'Managing the School as a Learning Organization' and 'Managing Equal Opportunities'. In summary, the overall programme is based on the following principles:

- individual commitment to professional development;
- individual readiness to take responsibility for their own learning;
- flexibility of method and content;
- the central role of school-based professional dialogue and reflective practice;
- the workplace as the learning environment;
- support from higher educational tutor, school management and colleagues who are students in the same school.

PROBLEMS OF IMPLEMENTATION AND LESSONS LEARNED

No single programme, however flexible or empowering, can ever claim to meet all professional development needs of school managers. This mode of flexible learning relies heavily on the communication of expertise through the printed word, and the consolidation of learning by means of interaction with colleagues and other learners. The authors delegate to tutors the responsibility for interaction, and this is primarily focused on the action research proposal and project rather than the ongoing process of working through the parts of the programme chosen by the students. Support from within the school is not always available, and when it is, it can be of varied quality and quantity. Intensive coaching for skills acquisition is not available as advocated in the literature on effective professional skills learning (Joyce and Showers, 1980; Oldroyd and Hall, 1991) but nevertheless, the materials and support provide many of the key elements at low cost which are needed in professional development. Evaluation studies of the implementation of the programme have pointed to many benefits for both individual managers and schools.

CONCLUSION

To shift the locus of control and responsibility to the individual manager and her or his own school can be seen as an empowering strategy used by the higher education provider. In its psychological usage, the term empowerment implies a strengthening of the self-esteem and confidence of the individual, as well as their scope for action. This school- and teacher-owned form of management self-development has sought, with some success, in both its approach and content to enhance the self-image and confidence of both managers and their schools.

Where there is a commitment to flexible learning located in the work setting, the culture of the workplace itself plays an important role in enhancing the process of empowerment. Evaluations of the University of Bristol programme (Quine, 1992; Hereford and Worcester, 1996) have identified the following conditions for a supportive context for empowerment through flexible learning:

- school managed development, particularly in the commissioning, planning and implementation of action research projects;

- organized peer group meetings to increase the opportunity for professional dialogue;
- provision of in-school time for study;
- strategic support from the local authority to provide continuity.

However, the following outcomes reported by programme participants testify to the efficacy of flexible learning for many: clarification of professional values; new confidence in management roles; increased participation in decision-making; improved performance at interview; better understanding of how to cope with and manage change; improved time management and team work. These are all aspects of the empowerment for which the flexible learning programme was designed. The testimony of one school manager of the programme offers strong encouragement for this mode of professional learning.

'We are of the firm belief that no other model of management development has achieved the impact on the *whole school* and *individual* level that this scheme has had. The use of action research as an integral component is of key importance. At the same time we had underestimated the critical importance of the "manager of action" and the demands on his time and expertise.' (Quine, 1992, p.3)

The above characteristics and the simple technology of print-based materials production have proved to be an 'intermediate technology' which has been implemented with minimal grant aid, and widely disseminated by a trained cadre of 44 facilitators throughout Poland (Oldroyd and Elsner, 1993). Over 7000 Polish school managers are now using the three original core units, and two specialist units have recently been produced by the Poles themselves.

REFERENCES

Department of Education and Science (1990) *Developing School Management: The Way Forward*, HMSO, London

Hereford and Worcester County Council (1996) *Management self-development in Hereford and Worcester Secondary Schools 1992–1995: Evaluation Report*, Hereford and Worcester County Council, Worcester

Joyce, B and Showers, B (1980) 'Improving Inservice Training: the Messages of Research, *Educational Leadership* February, pp. 379–85

Kolb, D A (1984) *Experiential Learning: Experience as a source of learning and development*, Prentice Hall, London

Oldroyd, D and Elsner, D (1993) 'Lessons in east–west collaboration in educational management' *Context* 4/93 pp. 16–17

Oldroyd, D and Hall, V (1991) *Managing Staff Development: A handbook for Secondary Schools*, Paul Chapman Publishers, London

Quine, K (1992) *NDCEMP/Berkshire Middle Management Development Project, Forest School*, Unpublished Evaluation Report

Schön, D (1983) *The Reflective Practitioner*, Basic Books, New York

Chapter 13

Off the Cuff and On the Cusp: A Flexible Approach to Teacher Development

Philip Garner and Chris Longman

This case study illustrates an attempt to meet the continuing professional development (CPD) needs of a primary school teacher through a distance learning modular programme. It emphasizes the importance of a collaborative approach to CPD, characterized by an intuitive response to client need, and underpinned by provider-flexibility.

INTRODUCTION

Distance learning programmes are becoming an integral part of the post-experience training portfolio of teachers. They already fulfil a crucial role in some aspects of teacher development in special educational needs (SEN), and their role is likely to become significant while teachers demand more choice and flexibility, and as traditional in-service training becomes inoperative because of cost and the inability of teachers to obtain release from school.

BACKGROUND

There has been growing concern that only a relatively small proportion of qualified teachers working mainly with children who have learning difficulties, possess a recognized additional qualification specifically related to special educational needs. The Special Educational Needs Training

Consortium (SENTC, 1996), for example, has noted that 46 per cent of teachers working with children who have severe learning difficulties had received no specialist training. This situation has arisen because of the negative impact of the changes in education following the 1988 Education Act, with teachers being faced with 'innovation overload', with little time to attend to professional development matters. Schools, too, have found it difficult to meet the cost of replacing teachers who attend day-time courses, resulting in an almost exclusive predominance of 'twilight' (late afternoon/early evening) courses at institutions of higher education. Moreover, as schools now operate in a market-governed education system, in which they control their own funds, CPD in SEN-related matters may be viewed as a low-priority need. Training arrangements also failed to take into account teacher mobility: given the significant investment of personal time and money, teachers now quite reasonably expect to have a 'portable' qualification, or part-qualification.

FLEXIBLE MODULAR COURSE PROVISION

This derives from an understanding of the factors which are currently inhibiting CPD in SEN. The course team has sought to provide flexible pathways to the awards of Postgraduate Diploma or Masters in SEN by providing:

- formal, taught modules in SEN and Severe Learning Difficulties (12 modules in total);
- distance learning packages in SEN and Severe Learning Difficulties (4 modules in total);
- accreditation of prior learning (APL) and accreditation of prior experiential learning (APEL), to a maximum of 50 per cent of the taught element of an award.

Using these, students have to complete eight modules (or the equivalent) for a postgraduate diploma, or 12 modules for a Masters degree in SEN (which includes a four-module equivalent dissertation). Each module amounts to 60 hours of study (including 20 hours of directed study) over a 15-week period.

It is the second of these which forms the subsequent focus of this account. For many years, teachers have felt that provision in CPD by higher education institutions has been out of touch with what went on in schools.

Moreover, the course team was aware that more needed to be done both to accommodate the pressures that teachers were working under, and to respond to the demand to make course content more applicable to what goes on in the classroom. Prior to this period of development, the CPD system had just one distance learning route, and accreditation of prior learning was in the early stages of development.

ONE TEACHER'S ROUTE

Margaret joined the CPD programme in September 1993, working towards a Masters degree in SEN. She taught in a local primary school, and at the outset she indicated her wish to obtain credit exemption for her 11 years previous experience as a teacher, and for SEN courses completed elsewhere. In order to do this she was given written guidance, and tutorial support, on the construction of two reflective statements: one related to her professional duties as a teacher, the other to courses she had followed at other institutions. With the former, Margaret compiled a detailed analysis of 1500 words, supported by school-based documentation, of a number of initiatives for which she had been responsible in her school. This was assessed, and one module exemption was allowed. In the case of her APL request, Margaret provided details of two SEN courses completed elsewhere during the last five years: both had been assessed by written assignment. Accordingly, in line with existing regulations, she was given two module exemptions. By the end of the 1993–4 academic year, after following three taught modules at the university, Margaret had thus completed six modules of the required eight taught modules.

In June 1994, however, Margaret obtained a promotion to Deputy Head of a primary school in the north of England, but she was keen to continue her studies at the university. Supervision of a subsequent Masters dissertation at a distance could be arranged, but before reaching this stage the university had to look at ways in which existing taught modules could be reconstituted as distance learning variants. Margaret had still to complete two compulsory modules, relating to curriculum differentiation and to management in SEN.

CONVERSION TO DISTANCE LEARNING

The course team, with the support of the course committee, set aside a block of time to rework the two traditionally delivered modules as distance learning packs. They were guided in this by a number of principles, which can apply to all distance learning courses.

Focus on the professional context

Each distance-based course should include an opportunity for the student to provide an account of the SEN provision in their new work situation. This included an opportunity for a student to reflect on SEN in his/her previous workplace and to make a reasoned comparison of the two.

Focus on a school-based SEN issue

Importantly, the new distance module included a focus on identifying a 'need' within SEN which had been identified after a student audit. In terms of a teacher new to a promoted post this was regarded to be vital, in that it (a) attended to an issue which required immediate action, and could therefore be viewed as locating the distance-learning endeavour in the real-life experience of the teacher, and (b) it would assist the student in dealing with an SEN matter of concern which would need their attention irrespective of any distance-learning obligations.

Self-contained learning material

There is a tendency, in some distance learning, to require students to have access to libraries and other resources. This was seen as a potentially inhibiting strategy, and contradictory to the spirit of 'distance' learning. Because the course team were all experienced authors, and had published widely on a range of matters relating to SEN, copyright issues were less problematic; this made provision of supporting material far easier to supply. Each of the two modules comprised seven points of focus, each with a main task and a series of supporting sub-tasks which could be adapted by individual students according to their own work situation. The tasks were to be written up in a module notebook, which constituted the assessed element. Each of the points of focus were supported by four readings.

Support for students

In the absence of any mechanism to support distance learning students, an agreed and suitably resourced strategy had to be found. In the case of tutor support this was to be accomplished by using traditional and more recent forms of information exchange (surface mail, telephone and facsimile, in the case of the former, and e-mail and Internet in the latter). Students studying at a distance have to have the reassurance that someone will be available to respond to queries, or to discuss issues as they arise, outside of more normal 'office' hours, when such students would be engaged in their studies. Students would be provided with a key weekday time and a key weekend time, during which they would know that the tutor would be available to answer queries by any of the electronic means outlined above.

Peer support was effected by circulating names and contact telephone numbers of other students pursuing distance modules; this was done only with the consent of the participants. There was, in addition, some discussion of the possibility of establishing an informal network of those institutions which provided distance learning in SEN, in order to expand this network of contacts.

On the basis of these principles, two distance learning packages were developed over a period of three months, enabling Margaret to begin work at the beginning of the Autumn term 1995. Her assignments for both modules were received on time and were regarded to be of Masters level in quality.

MARGARET'S EXPERIENCE: AN EVALUATORY SUMMARY

Margaret contacted her tutor 14 times during the 15 week duration of the module. Of these contacts four were by letter, one was by fax and the remaining nine were by telephone. Only one of the telephone calls was made outside a key time, and only one was made at a key time during a weekend. Three of the contacts were made regarding procedural matters: these related to clarification or further guidance on the content of the distance learning package. The remainder of the contacts concerned discussions regarding aspects of SEN, related either to the individual tasks or to the layout of the final (notebook) assignment.

In Margaret's opinion the modules were largely successful: 'I have been able to continue, uninterrupted, my Masters course, and I don't think I could have stomached getting to grips with a new university.' She felt that the focus of the modules was about right, giving her 'A lot of information, but being quite challenging to me about my new school. It made me analyse what I was new to, without falling into the trap of a "grass is greener" mentality.' None the less, Margaret did identify some weaknesses of the approach, notably that, as one of the first students to attempt the new format, there was little opportunity for peer support.

There are now approximately 20 distance learning students following the two modules described in this case study, and the course team are investigating the possibility of expanding the scheme. It is also likely that the distance learning variants will be incorporated within a newly developing MA in Comparative Special Education, involving partner institutions from elsewhere in Europe, its development being funded in part by the European Community's Socrates and Youth Programme.

REFERENCES

Special Educational Needs Training Consortium (1996) *Professional Development to Meet Special Educational Needs*, SENTC, Stafford

Chapter 14

Flexible Learning in Modular Programmes for Professional Studies

Lyn Shipway

This case study describes the design of an open learning framework comprising a number of resource-based modules, leading to a diploma for post-registration nurses and midwives. Modules are mainly designed around existing resources which students purchase direct from the publishers. Comprehensive module guidelines have been prepared by the module leader. A successful pilot has been completed with European students.

INTRODUCTION

There have been radical reforms in nurse and midwifery education following a series of reports (United Kingdom Central Council for Nurses, Midwives and Health Visitors (UKCC) 1986; Royal College of Nursing (RCN) 1985; English National Board for Nursing Midwifery and Health Visiting (ENB) 1985). All pre-registration programmes now lead to a diploma in higher education, with full student status. A subsequent UKCC report', The Report on the Post-Registration Education and Practice Project' (PREPP) recommended that all registered nurses provide evidence of lifelong learning (UKCC, 1990).

The major challenges to post-registration nursing and midwifery education are:

- UKCC post-registration regulations require all qualified nurses and midwives to provide evidence of current learning for re-registration every three years.

- The existence of a significant number of qualified nursing staff (500,000 potential students) who have not studied in recent years but who now wish to access undergraduate study as they are facilitating both diplomates and graduate nurses in the workplace.
- A professional and local need for work-based learning programmes.
- Students geographically dispersed over a wide area.
- The need to offer professionally recognized programmes accompanied by a reduction in the numbers of specialist lecturers throughout the schools.
- Many potential students have to study part-time, in their own time, and are self-funded.
- Health Trust purchasers demand value for money and flexible programmes which will occasion minimal disruption to their workforce.
- The need of the school to compete with other educational providers for business.
- A commitment to the development of inter-professional programmes of study.
- A commitment to the development of modules which are dual accredited by professional bodies, the University and, in some instances by the National Council for Vocational Qualification (NCVQ).

Open learning, while having no definitive definition, is generally accepted by educators to be a philosophical approach to learning in which the student needs are paramount. Barriers to learning are minimized, giving students greater choice in:

- what to learn;
- how to learn (methods, media, etc);
- where that learning should take place;
- when to learn;
- modes of assessment.

(Adapted from the work of Lewis and Spencer, 1986, cited in Robinson 1989, p.23.)

PILOT PROJECT

A pilot project was established to develop a selection of resource-based modules providing nursing and midwifery students choice in the mode of study, the level of support required, the level of learning and the assessment schedule. The modules are offered at certificate, diploma and degree level, either as stand-alone modules, or as part of a designated pathway to established awards.

The initial stage of the project was to design an open learning framework identifying the requisite operational structures, quality assurance mechanisms, and administrative procedures. Consultation with the university academic standards committee and senior school staff ensured the framework complied with university and professional regulations.

The majority of the modules are offered at both academic levels; the student is given the choice of three assessment dates over an 18-month period; all of the modules include a minimal two hours personal tutorial time, with the inclusion of optional study days for selected modules. This degree of flexibility has enabled us to meet the needs of small numbers of students for whom an alternative is not available.

One module, the 'Independent Learning Module (ILM)', offers maximum flexibility, with the students negotiating their level of study, their chosen learning outcomes, the manner in which they will achieve the outcomes and the way in which they will present for assessment. This module is particularly popular with clinical practitioners as it allows them to acquire learning in a clinical speciality which would otherwise be unavailable to them. Eighteen undergraduates from our Malaysian outcentre successfully completed this module in December 1996.

An early decision was made to adopt, adapt, or author new materials in that order, thus maximizing available resources (Race, 1994). Nursing and midwifery are fortunate in that a number of organizations produce high quality learning materials designed specifically for health studies. Therefore, the majority of the modules are designed around existing resources and further supported by comprehensive module guides authored by a university module leader. Where the materials require adaptation, this has been achieved by producing an extended module guide with additional reading and further student activities.

The successful pilot of a module, 'The Emotional Effects of Childbirth' was completed in December 1996. The materials were purchased from a professional organization, the module was offered either at a distance, or with two supporting study days, with all students having a predetermined entitlement to personal tutor time. Eight students completed the module including the two supported study days, with a further three students opting for the distance mode. Both alternatives were positively evaluated by students and lecturers.

To date, lecturers have authored two 'in-house' learning packages and we anticipate that others will be available shortly. In particular, staff are focusing on the development of resources to support specialist clinical subject areas not incorporated within the School's existing portfolio, thus enabling students to access learning unavailable in the traditional mode.

For example, the subject of facilitating survivors of domestic violence and sexual assault, while recognized as a need by professional nurses and midwives, is as yet not high on the educational agenda. Operating a traditional taught module would not be cost-effective due to the limited demand for the specialist subject, and the paucity of UK subject literature, particularly in relation to men's issues. An open learning package was created with much of the supporting literature procured from the Internet. This module is now available for study either at a distance or with an optional two study days, and costing varies according to the delivery mode.

In February 1997, a European pilot study utilizing these written resources commenced. Students are supported by a combination of five video-conferencing sessions with ongoing academic debate via computer-conferencing, and personal tutor support.

CONCLUSION

It became obvious from open learning enquiries, that the majority of potential students required a structured route to a diploma award. For this reason a major launch of the initial project was delayed until the team had designed a designated award-bearing programme achievable primarily through open learning.

The planned programme optimizes flexibility by including a combination of accreditation of prior (experiential) learning (AP(E)L), open learning modules, traditional taught modules, independent learning modules, and learning from other higher education institutions. Each student designs, in conjunction with the pathway leader, an individual learning plan to ensure an integrated learning experience. Levels of learning, completion dates and support are negotiated in accordance with university and professional regulations, between the individual student and the pathway leader.

Development costs have been minimized, with students purchasing most of the supporting materials direct from the publishers, and to date module leaders have been recruited from existing staff, with the student support being integrated into their ongoing workload. With increased demand it is anticipated that part-time lecturers will be employed, utilizing monies generated from the open learning initiative.

For the first year it has been considered necessary for the teaching and learning advisor to act as pathway leader and open learning coordinator to ensure parity of learning for all students. It was anticipated that open learning students might have divergent needs that differed to those of traditional students, and that few supporting lecturers at that time had the appropriate experience. By taking overall responsibility for supporting both lecturers and students, the teaching and learning advisor could anticipate and meet the needs of both groups. It is anticipated that after the first year new students will be incorporated into existing pathways, following staff development in facilitating open learning students.

REFERENCES

English National Board for Nursing, Midwifery and Health Visiting (ENB) (1985)
   Professional Education and Training courses, Consultation Paper, ENB, London
Robinson, K (1989) *Open and Distance Learning for Nurses*, Longman Group, London
Race, P (1994) *The Open Learning Handbook*, 2nd edn, Kogan Page, London
Royal College of Nursing (RCN) (1985) *The Education of Nurses: a new dispensation*,
   Commission on Nursing, RCN, London
United Kingdom Central Council for Nursing, Midwifery and Health Visiting (UKCC)
   (1986) *Project 2000: A new preparation for practice*, UKCC, London
United Kingdom Central Council for Nursing, Midwifery and Health Visiting (UKCC)
   (1990) *The Report on the Post-Registration Education and Practice Project*, UKCC, London

Chapter 15

A Flexible Programme in Applied Studies in Education and Training

Andrina McCormack

Northern College is an Institute of Higher Education based in Dundee and Aberdeen. The Postgraduate Diploma in Applied Studies in Education and Training programme has been running since 1994. It is based heavily on the former Diploma in Educational Technology which ran successfully for over twenty years as a distance learning course. Within the programme, students who are all in full-time employment may decide to complete related certificate awards (four modules) in open learning, materials production, course design or professional development. Each module, certificate and the diploma are credit rated towards the Masters programme.

INTRODUCTION

The majority of students taking the Postgraduate Diploma in Applied Studies in Education and Training (DASET) are teachers from all sectors, from primary through to higher education, but there is a substantial proportion of trainers in health and social services, the United Kingdom (UK) armed services and the Portuguese Navy, and from industry. There are students from across the UK, Europe and North America, and occasions have arisen when we have provided on-campus accommodation for students supported by the British Council, who complete their distance learning materials in college, with face-to-face tutorial contact, but do so full time, thus drastically reducing their completion time. Because of the variety of demands on students' time, the underlying philosophy of the course emphasizes flexibility backed up with strong tutorial support.

ACCESS TO THE PROGRAMME

DASET is open to experienced trainers, teachers and educationalists, who may or may not be qualified to degree level. What is important is that students have a strong experience on which to draw, and to which to relate their studies at postgraduate level. We therefore have a 'two year experience' clause for prospective candidates.

Registration is on a monthly, roll-on roll-off basis, so students may start at the beginning of any month of the year, and complete at their own pace, given a notional completion time of three months per module, eighteen months for a certificate, and four years for the diploma. Extensions may be granted where students give sound personal or professional extenuating circumstances.

ACCESS TO KNOWLEDGE AND UNDERSTANDING

The course is at postgraduate level, and modular in structure, covering areas including:

- learning;
- assessment;
- delivery;
- evaluation;
- course design;
- appraisal and development of study materials;
- theory and management of open learning;
- materials production.

Because of the generic nature of the course in both its philosophy and practice, it is equally applicable for nursery teachers as for commanders in the Portuguese Navy. Its strength lies in the emphasis that generic theories and principles should be demonstrably applied within the student's own work context. Assignments are thus designed in order that students may do this.

TUTOR SUPPORT

Great emphasis is put on the quality of tutorial support, and a customized handbook for tutors is issued to all tutors. Race (1989) suggests that the role of tutor involves three major responsibilities:

- **tutoring** – providing tuition either face-to-face or at a distance;
- **assessing** – marking assignments and providing advice and guidance;
- **counselling** – giving more general support and guidance.

Rowntree (1986) proposes the following as key roles in tutorial support:

- encouraging/supporting the learner;
- discussing particular difficulties;
- mapping out the course;
- guiding practical work
- advising on options;
- giving guidance on study methods;
- marking and commenting.

The tutor not only supports the learning materials or explains difficult points but also acts as a sounding board against which students can bounce ideas in order to develop new trains of thought, expand existing concepts, and identify new strategies.

STUDENT RESPONSIBILITIES

The student responsibilities are outlined in the course handbook issued as part of the induction package. They are responsible for keeping tutors informed as to progress, submitting any drafts or assignments within the target dates, and negotiating extensions if required. The students are expected to treat their tutor as a professional colleague. They should respect the integrity of the tutorial relationship, and while they may not always take advice, then they should reflect on it and make a considered decision before ignoring it.

Students are responsible for their own learning and control the pace, timing and quality of their study. Postgraduate-level study brings together many personal, professional and academic quoteualities in individuals, and can, perhaps should, make challenging demands on their resources.

DASET students should be able to demonstrate:

- implementation of theory, including knowledge, skills and understanding, as applied to practice;

- sound analytical skills;

- objective and impartial reasoning and judgement;

- extrapolation of theory from practice;

- the ability to analyse and evaluate critically both strategies and materials as used in their own training/educational context.

Personal qualities required include a commitment to change and improvement in professional activity, through the resolution of professional problems. DASET students are expected to bring realistic and pragmatic solutions derived from practice and experience, with academic rigour and intellectual and professional integrity, born of experience, and as a reflective practitioner.

STRUCTURAL SUPPORT

A variety of mechanisms are available:

- A modular structure to ensure choice – students may combine optional modules from an extensive bank to form a study programme of their choice to match their own interests and needs.

- A study package approach to ensure flexibility – students work through at a time, pace and place to suit themselves, packages of distance learning study materials including printed units, video cassettes, computer software, readings, books and practical activities as appropriate for individual modules.

- Tutorial support to ensure active learning – warm, supportive and professional tutorial support is the linchpin of delivery and success in DASET.

- Online communication to ensure interaction – e-mail and computer conferencing are provided free, although students must have access to a modem to make use of these optional services. Conferencing allows sharing and collaboration with fellow participants as well as tutors.

- Integral assessment to ensure relevance – formative and summative assessment tasks are included throughout the modules. The formative activities highlight important aspects of learning. Most summative assignments comprise three parts, the first two addressing the application of theory into practice, while the third requires students to reflect back on their own learning process throughout the study of the module just completed.

- Partnership to ensure purposeful development – the student's own personal and professional expertise works in partnership with the study process. The partnership between students and tutors develops as an interaction for learning. Students are encouraged to be active learners who seek out opportunities for personal and professional development.

- Participant support groups to combat isolation – students are encouraged to set up local study groups. However, as DASET is a totally distance learning programme, an optional study day is held once per term, which offers both a tailored programme and the opportunity to meet up with staff and other students.

The very nature of flexible learning at a distance places an onus on students to be responsible for their rate of progress, often in the most trying circumstances. The DASET programme encourages students to customize their study through the tasks they undertake, and the opportunities to choose at least some elements of their programme.

In a study on motivation and the distant student, McCormack (1994) found that students liked the flexible nature of DASET, and used the following support mechanisms:

- Professional and personal support – most respondents noted the support of a valued colleague or friend as self-help support, and many remarked on the support of their partner or spouse.

- Allocated study location and time – students reported allocating specific time and study space. This 'location in space' seemed to legitimize their taking time out to pursue their studies.

- College support – it was clearly evident that college support was of lesser significance than local peer and personal support in flexible distance learning.

These results confirm other findings (McCombs, 1991; Drummond and Croll, 1983; Kinzie, 1990; Reeve, 1989) that motivation in distance learning is based primarily on intrinsic factors inherent to the individual learner, but that personal networks of support are more important than those provided by the institution delivering the award.

LIBRARY SUPPORT FOR A VARIETY OF MATERIALS

Access is available to all library materials and open access facilities including computers, photocopiers, microfiche and CD-ROM, by mail and on-site where appropriate.

CONCLUSION

Students' previous education may not have equipped them to cope with the independence and self-discipline demanded by open and flexible learning. Tutors need therefore to facilitate autonomy and independence, considering students' opinions and approaches which may conflict with their own.

Flexible and open learning is the way forward in a world where students are drawn from a wide age-range, varying background, both in the UK and overseas, and perhaps experiencing tremendous social, personal and economic pressures.

Where students can be supported to take control and responsibility for their own learning, with tutors as 'an authority', rather than 'in authority' (Peters, 1972), then immense and profound personal and professional development can take place to contribute to the development of individuals, their organization and the wider society.

REFERENCES

Drummond, R J and Croll J C (1983) 'Intrinsic and Extrinsic Motivation and Attitudes Toward Professional Continuing Education: Implications for the Counsellors', *Journal of Employment Counselling* 20, pp. 88–96

Kinzie, M B (1990) 'Requirements and Benefits of Effective Interactive Instruction: Learner Control, Self-Regulation and Continuing Motivation' *Educational Technology Research and Development*, 38, pp. 5–21

McCombs, B L (1991) 'Unravelling Motivation' *Journal of Experimental Education*, 60, pp. 3–88

McCormack, A E (1994) 'Interactivity at a Distance – Motivation and the Distant Learner' in: Foot H C *et al.* (eds) *Group and Interactive Learning*, Computational Mechanics Publications, Southampton pp. 99–103

Peters, R S (1972) *Ethics and Education*, Allen and Unwin, London

Race, P (1989) *The Open Learning Handbook*, Kogan Page, London

Reeve, J (1989) 'Intrinsic Motivation and the Acquisition and Maintenance of Four Experiential States' *Journal of Social Psychology*, 129, pp. 841–54

Rowntree, D (1986) *Teaching Through Self Instruction*, Kogan Page, London

SECTION III
Flexible Approaches to Skills Development

INTRODUCTION

The case studies in this section demonstrate the need for flexible approaches to skills development in higher education. Cock and Pickard (Chapter 16) talk of a paradigm shift in this area from traditional modes of delivery, aimed at transmission of knowledge, to more flexible approaches which take into account the diversity of student experience and background. They are involved in providing access to higher education and focus on the development of number skills. They have created an environment for students to study and acquire mathematical skills.

This is followed by a case study from Ure (Chapter 17) in Scotland where non-traditional students create a profile. The aim of the profile is to demonstrate evidence of learning which can be used as a skills passport that provides evidence of learning and transferable skills to future employers. Gillies-Denning (Chapter 18) describes an access to higher education programme which targets non-traditional learners and is delivered in the students' community. This example illustrates the importance of not re-inventing the wheel, and draws on experience from the United States of America. The same course also utilizes students to act as mentors for other students.

Macauley and Pagnucci (Chapter 19) consider a writing skills course for non-traditional students. The cost of education and fees for students is a key issue in most countries. Their course stimulates students to negotiate their own learning; in addition they access e-mail and the World Wide Web to complete assignments and develop portfolios. Bingham and Drew (Chapter 20) describe the use of SkillPacks for students which develop transferable skills which can be used both in the university and in the student's place of future employment. The SkillPacks have been developed and published with both international and external markets in mind.

Bainbridge (Chapter 21) discusses the development of a library skills study pack for engineering students. It has a hands-on approach and allows the students to develop their information seeking skills – skills for life. The project has been evaluated. Finally, Steward (Chapter 22) discusses a project specifically developed for use by postgraduate students which involves utilizing the campus computer network. It involves the students taking responsibility for their own learning as well as developing transferable skills.

Chapter 16

Flexible Maths

Sybil Cock and Poppy Pickard

The University of North London is committed to serving the needs of local communities and in particular those groups who have historically been excluded from higher education, such as women and members of ethnic minorities. The university has a long tradition of providing courses suited to mature returners to education, and was one of the original instigators of access courses in the early 1980s. In the late 1980s as part of a government initiative to attract more people into science and technology, the university introduced a Higher Introductory Technology and Engineering Conversion Course (HITECC). This now serves as a foundation course, which provides a year zero for the University's Bachelor in Science modular degree scheme. This includes degree titles as diverse as human nutrition and dietetics, to business decision analysis and communications. The flexible maths unit is the first compulsory unit on this science foundation course.

WHY WE NEED A FLEXIBLE APPROACH

Our task was to design this unit in such a way that it could flexibly accommodate the needs of large numbers of students from an unpredictable range of mathematical backgrounds. The students are mature returners together with school or college leavers with disappointing advanced level and other results; thus there is a mix of motivations and attitudes towards study, as well as a wide mix of levels of attainment and confidence. Besides these behavioural attributes, the students also have a wide range of previous learning in mathematics. Some students would be meeting topics for the first time, others for the second or third time – in which case it may simply be a case of brushing up and refreshing their knowledge. Sometimes the rather more difficult task of unravelling and reconstructing something that has not been fully digested in the first place is called for.

Our own experiences as teachers were formed on further education access courses and in schools, and are heavily influenced by a student-centred nurturing pedagogy, which encourages students to become active learners, and in this capacity make sense of mathematical concepts and apply them in a variety of situations and contexts. Central to this approach is that of confidence-building. This contrasts, often quite starkly, with the dominant pedagogy of mathematics in higher education, which is based on a transmission or instructional model of learning; lecturing, and which presupposes a uniformity of mathematical attainment from students at the beginning of the course.

There is widespread recognition that mathematics is a big source of anxiety to many people, and students often present highly negative feelings about their past classroom experiences in the subject. In his seminal book, *Do You Panic about Maths?* Buxton's (1981) central message to the student is; 'to reflect upon how you are functioning when you are learning. It was through the process of asking people to say what was happening and what they felt, that they obtained some release in their ability to tackle maths'(p.99). Our strategy was to incorporate as many opportunities as we could for confidence building activities, and to emphasize frequently the benefits of metacognitive and reflective activities.

The recent expansion in total student numbers, the declining unit of resource, the development of modular degrees which offer an attractively wide choice of study programmes, have all meant that introductory mathematics courses must now be provided on a larger scale. Thus the first year of our experiment saw a total of around 100 students, in any context a substantial administrative challenge.

We were concerned to design the course in such a way that the very scarce staff resources could be used in a highly focused way to provide students with assistance, dialogue and guidance on the issues and topics where it was most needed, rather than 'telling' a large and diverse group of students things they might already know, or, alternatively, might be in no position to assimilate.

Our flexible maths experiment also acknowledged important features of the new student body. The declining real value of the student grant means that many more students have part-time jobs. The trend towards studying near to home is particularly marked at institutions such as ours. Many University of North London students cannot count on the traditional student study environment, perhaps epitomized by the hall of residence study-bedroom. The University's learning centre, and the maths workshop within it, provide an important place to study for our students. This comfortable and welcoming environment has become an established workplace for HITECC students who could often be found outside workshop hours collaborating around the large tables.

HOW THE COURSE IS RUN

Teaching materials for this unit were based around a study guide and eleven topic booklets. The study guide provided all the organizational information about the unit together with hints on how to study, specific references to additional materials for each topic which were readily accessible in the workshop area, and profiling pages which encouraged the students to reflect on their learning and determine their own targets. The inevitably complex assessment procedures were also detailed. The 11 booklets contained the mathematical content, which includes: arithmetic, linear and quadratic algebra, indices, trigonometry and graphs.

The material was presented in a variety of ways: using common signposts; individual and group activities; investigations; exposition; worked examples; exercises; supporting software and self-assessment tests. Writing the materials was a major task; the resource implications of the initiative in terms of staff time should not be underestimated. The University makes small amounts of money available to fund projects such as these; in practice each of us was given the equivalent of one day a week's teaching relief for one semester to develop the materials. They are, of course, the subject of constant revision!

The unit was delivered completely through supported open learning workshops which were staffed by between one and three tutors depending on the anticipated student demand. Workshop sessions were run for these students on three mornings a week, for three hours. Other subject commitments meant each student was potentially free to attend for two of these mornings, offering a maximum of six hours access to learning support. The maths workshop area provided a mathematically richly resourced environment with a text book collection, some available on library loan, access to additional handouts, plus two computers which could be used with graph plotting software.

We are fully aware that assessment is a major motivator to learning, and designed the assessment schedule so that it would support flexibility. We allowed students to take each of the four assessments at any time over a period of several weeks, and individual feedback was available at the next workshop session. This allowed students to repeat any assessment if they felt they could improve their mark. Although the pass mark for any unit was 40 per cent we encouraged students to aim for 60 per cent as the material they were studying would provide the foundation for much future work. Two rooms which lead off the workshop area were used for untimed assessments. Students and tutors adopted a fairly relaxed manner about using these rooms to start and finish assessments.

We made it clear to students that the unit organization was designed to enable them to succeed at mathematics by developing ownership of the underlying concepts. We did not see mathematics as a set of techniques or rules to be learned, but as a language with a logical structure that repeated itself in many different situations. This understanding was imperative, since, as impending scientists and technologists our cohort would be very dependent on developing an acuity with mathematics. Staff were there to provide individual and small-group help, addressing the questions posed by students rather than delivering recipes on how to do it. Within this framework students were able to:

- work collaboratively and realize that mathematics is something you discuss in order to understand;

- work at their own pace, often working on two booklets at once in order to devote extra effort to a new topic of difficulty without letting it hold them back;

- develop ownership of mathematical concepts through discussion and investigative work, thus meeting the challenge of 're-learning' something that was never fully understood;

- devote less time to more familiar topics and more time to new topics;

- receive affirmation and encouragement about their own understanding both from tutors and peers;

- check on their own progress and decide when they were ready to be tested;

- take the tests in a relaxed and informal atmosphere, removing any fear that this was a now-or-never event;

- plan their work and attendance around their personal commitments.

CONCLUSION

Groups of students were interviewed twice during the course by an external evaluator. From these evaluations, there was a developing feeling that this way of working was preferable to taught classes followed by tutorial sessions. Students liked working from the booklets, and learning from each other in group sessions. A significant minority of students requested more formal input – undoubtedly some students were not at ease with the amount of responsibility given to them and wanted the comfort of lectures.

Inevitably, the biggest question about flexible maths is 'did exam results improve?' It is very difficult to measure this as we did not have a control group studying foundation maths in a more formal manner. However, comparing end results with initial diagnostic marks showed that the majority of students benefited from the course, some showing quite dramatic improvement.

We hope we have created a course, and a learning environment, which provides a rich range of mathematical stimuli from which students can construct mathematical meanings.

REFERENCE

Buxton, Laurie (1981) *Do You Panic about Maths?*, Heinemann Educational, London

Chapter 17

Profiling Study and Communication Styles for Non-Traditional Students

Jenny Ure

The Centre for Continuing Education at Aberdeen University recently piloted a profile for study, communication and survival skills as part of a personal development plan for the large cohort of non-traditional students on the Aberdeen University Summer School for Access. This benefited from funding from the University Centre for Educational Development, and builds on the evidence of nationally funded research on the value of core skills in successful transition to/and progression in degree study (Cudworth and Ure, 1997).

WHY PROFILING?

Where needs are many and varied, where resources are scarce and where failure is costly to both parties, it seems logical to ensure that the resources of students, staff and organizations are effectively targeted on key needs.

Profiling rests on the assumption that educational performance can benefit from the harnessing of effort towards priority needs, and provision of opportunities to share skills, strategies and criteria (Tomlinson and Kilner, 1991). The same process in organizational contexts is evident in 'benchmarking' (Weller, 1996).

Profiling contributes to the quality of teaching and learning by:

- clarifying shared criteria and objectives;
- identifying priority needs to meet these objectives;

- sharing strategies and targeting resources in these key areas of need;
- documenting achievements for accreditation in different institutions.

Whether the process is applied to a single course, to a long-term career plan, or to a school or company audit, it is designed to help students, tutors/trainers and training organizations answer the same key questions in pursuit of personal, professional or organizational development in an increasingly competitive market.

- Where are we now?
- Where do we need to be?
- How are we going to get there?
- What are the next steps?

Students, tutors, departments and organizations differ in the speed and adequacy with which they identify and meet the requirements of their changing market. Profiling, as part of a personal and professional development plan (PDP), offers a framework for this process.

WHY CORE STUDY AND COMMUNICATION SKILLS?

According to a European Commission report (1991), a key feature of the 'skills gap' now emerging is the widespread lack of important generic skills and social skills (such as problem-solving skills, learning skills and communication skills), which mediate the ability of companies to operate across national and cultural boundaries.

In an increasingly competitive and international market, new personal and professional skills are increasingly at a premium (Higher Education for Capability, 1993). These core skills, and new professional ones, are increasingly being acquired as a part of lifelong learning in different contexts. Where learning ceases to be a function of a particular institution, there is a need for a document that will accompany the learner, and conflate a number of institutional and pedagogical functions. The PDP or 'Skills Passport' is likely to be that document, (Confederation of British Industry (CBI) 1995).

The profiling pilot evaluated in this paper builds on the evidence for the academic role of core skills from a large, nationally funded research project

(Scottish Higher Education Funding Council, 1997), which highlights the importance of a range of skills.

Core skills:
- study and communication skills;
- problem-solving skills;
- personal organizational skills;
- IT skills.

Core needs:
- feedback;
- confidence;
- knowing what is expected.

WHY NON-TRADITIONAL STUDENTS?

From the point of view of academic or organizational cost-effectiveness, there are strong reasons for ensuring that core skills are profiled as part of a formal PDP. With current staff:student ratios, limited tutorial contact and large groups of students from different classes and cultures, the social and academic network can no longer be relied upon to clarify what is expected of them, or how it can be achieved.

This is particularly disadvantageous for students from non-professional backgrounds, whose social or academic background might not compensate for the reduction of institutional support and feedback as tutor:student ratios decline. Profiling tutors' expectations as part of a portfolio makes criteria more explicit to students, tutors and other institutions. In addition to this, it offers a means of harnessing tutor, student and institutional resources more effectively towards them.

THE PILOT PROJECT

The pilot project was carried out with the 1996 cohort of the Aberdeen University summer school as an integral part of their ten-week intensive access programme. Over one hundred students took part in the pilot, together with six tutors who participated in two training and development sessions with the materials prior to the start of the course in June. They used the profiles in three one-to-one sessions (tutor-assisted learning), and also as an integral part of group work (peer-assisted learning), and individual work (resource-assisted learning).

How useful was profiling/action planning?

Questionnaires and interviews were used to generate quantitative and qualitative evidence on the general usefulness of such profiling and action planning. The key focus was on profiling as a means of:

- clarifying what is expected of students;
- identifying key problems early;
- addressing these problems collaboratively.

Eighty per cent of students found it useful to a greater or lesser extent, and of the 20 per cent recorded as nil responses, 14 per cent indicated that this was not because it had been unhelpful, but because the tutor had not used it with them. The response reflects experience not only of the materials, but the way these were used by tutors as a means of constructive feedback, and collaborative forward planning.

Some strengths and weaknesses identified by students

Helps clarify what is expected:

> 'Insight into problem areas that you may not have noticed.'

> 'It spells out exactly what is required.'

Helps identify problems:

> 'Helped me identify key problem areas.'

> 'Helped me understand where I was going wrong.'

Helps address problems:

> 'It made me identify problems and take care in the future.'

> 'It gave a structure to work to/a structure to work on improving my work.'

TEACHING ISSUES

Action planning was also identified as a useful vehicle of communication, highlighting the inter-dependent roles of teacher, learner and institution in mediating academic performance. This can be a double-edged sword if there is not real commitment to supporting the process, as it raises expectations that tutors can and will rise to the challenge, and that time and resources will be facilitated by the department if necessary.

'Problem areas were identified too late.'

'You would have to get proper teaching and less chat.'

'We did not get any advice/tackle the problems.'

'When you have a problem it takes more than action planning to get rid of it.'

In some cases students describe a more informal profiling and action planning process with their tutors which clearly fulfilled many of these functions, yet was seen as separate (and even in opposition to) the formalized concept.

Many tutors felt that the students were already in small supportive groups, with a much more natural tutor/student interface, but recognized that the process could be very important in the large anonymous context of many undergraduate courses, particularly in the case of resource-based learning.

Resources

While raising expectations is central to raising the standards of teaching and learning, there were resource implications which tutors and departments were not able to meet. It is at this interface that the commitment of the department or the institution is likely to be a significant factor.

Skills

Effective tutors in negotiated teaching and learning are identified as approachable, empathic, and hard on problems rather than on people (Francis, 1991). Not all tutors fit neatly into that slot, and there may be an argument for using other students, or more experienced peers in this role, where the balance of power is more evenly distributed.

Format

It was difficult to find a balance between too much detail in the profile and too little. The solution adopted was to use a simple model as a springboard for discussion in more detail with tutor and student.

Benefits

The study outlined here confirms that the profiling process can enhance provision and performance by highlighting the changing needs of a heterogeneous student cohort, and targeting shrinking resources more effectively and coherently to meet them.

The profile helped:

- ensure earlier awareness of unsuspected gaps or problems;
- clarify teaching and learning objectives and marking criteria;
- provide a basis for discussion of and reflection on how to address problems;
- highlight gaps in the curriculum, the teaching, the learning and the resources.

This approach has been adopted in full or in part in other access and induction courses in the University. It matches the corresponding profiles of performance in core skills now being implemented with school and college based applicants to university and fulfils the need for feedback, support and clarity so clearly evident from our research on the variables affecting non-traditional students preparing for higher education.

CONCLUSION

Organizations such as the CBI (1995), and the European Commission (1991), have consistently made the case for the need for a framework for personal, professional and organizational development which both facilitates and records progression as part of lifelong learning.

Profiling core skills as part of a professional development plan offers a viable means of achieving this for the hundreds of students who enter each year through the summer access programmes at Scottish universities.

REFERENCES

Confederation of British Industry (1995) *Realising the Vision: a skills passport*, CBI

Cudworth, C and Ure, J (1997 pending) *Alterable Variables in Academic Achievement*, Scottish Higher Education Funding Council Research Report

European Commission (1991) *Memorandum on Higher Education in the European Community*, European Community Task Force on Human Resources, Education, Training and Youth

Higher Education for Capability (1993) *Student Skills for the New Europe*, HEC Conference Report (ed L Cunningham) HEC, Leeds

Tomlinson, P and Kilner, S (1991) *The Flexible Learning Framework and Current Educational Theory*, Employment Department, Sheffield

Weller, L D (1996) 'Benchmarking: a paradigm for change to quality education' *TQM journal.* 8 (6) pp. 24–9

Chapter 18

Flexibility in Teaching and Learning Schemes

Philip Gillies-Denning

This Queen Margaret College (QMC) project sought to develop an 'accessible curriculum' at higher education level 1, which would create a learning environment to enable learners from socially and educationally disadvantaged groups (such as long-term unemployed, disabled people, people from minority ethnic communities), in peripheral urban areas of North Edinburgh, to realize their educational potential. The pilot phase of the 'accessible curriculum' project ran from October 1994 to June 1996 and involved three modules within the combined studies programme.

INTRODUCTION

In educational sectoral terms, the project has sought to provide articulation between higher education and successful community-based community education providers. The rationale behind this connection is that with an increasing intake into higher education of non-standard students who face the situational, institutional and dispositional barriers identified by Cross (1986) and McGivney (1990), any successful attempt at articulation between these two sectors must capitalize on and adapt to the higher education environment; good existing practices pioneered and evolved by various community education projects in the United Kingdom and abroad; and in recruitment, teaching, curriculum construction, learning and support for under-represented groups. The project, as a *partner in educational progression* has worked closely with people, projects and agencies already providing educational opportunities (both from the public and voluntary sector) for the target group in North Edinburgh.

AIMS AND OBJECTIVES OF THE PROJECT

Aims

- To work actively with local projects such as 'Second Chance to Learn' (2CTL), to develop a means of identifying, targeting and encouraging those adults who would benefit from higher education but who lack traditional entry qualifications.

- To develop three year-1 modules within the QMC Combined Studies programme which will specifically act as 'orientation' modules and incorporate, where possible, aspects of the Adult Career Counselling: Education and Support Services (ACCESS) integrated model from the College Of New Rochelle, School of New Resources (SNR), New York City, USA.

- To develop, with current QMC staff, the skills necessary to work with adult learners from the target group.

Objectives

- To select and develop, with key personnel within QMC and outside agencies, the strategies and techniques required to facilitate an 'accessible curriculum' programme for and into higher education.

- To identify and develop resource material, both with outside agencies and in-house.

- To establish the curriculum content, learning outcomes and assessment strategies for such a programme, and develop new modules where necessary, which can then be validated and piloted.

- To deliver such a programme in the local community, using QMC staff and community education professionals.

- To monitor and assess the effectiveness of the programme and student outcomes.

PROGRAMME DEVELOPMENT

This involved, through the auspices of 2CTL, discussing the project with potential learners and staff. It became clear that academic and personal guidance were of key importance and would have to be integrated into the curriculum since both staff and students were apprehensive about the move from a community based programme into higher education in terms of the support services required.

Community education professionals and potential students identified three key areas that any programme would have to address:

- learning support;

- structural support;

- personal support.

As a result, the programme was constructed around these three key areas. Students further identified the disciplines of sociology and psychology as areas of academic interest, since these built on previous work undertaken by the students in the community based projects.

The project coordinator, using aspects of the pioneering College of New Rochelle, School of New Resources ACCESS programme that could cross the cultural divide, began work to construct the programme that would address these three key areas.

LEARNING SUPPORT

It proved possible for existing and experienced QMC staff to adapt the existing level 1 combined studies module on 'Study Skills' for the target group. Adaptation by the project coordinator of one ACCESS module ('Experience, Learning, Identity') resulted in a module that would fit the Scottish target group. This new module, 'Individual, Family, Society: 1' was developed to take account of and develop the adult learners' critical reflection and understanding of existing and previous educational experiences, and the coping and resistance strategies that may result from them.

Following discussions with potential students, who identified access to the career structures within the wider Edinburgh urban labour market as a goal, it was further decided to construct another module entitled 'Place, Work, Folk: 1'. This module took its approach and title from the work and theories of the pioneering Edinburgh thinker in environmental (in its widest sense) education, Sir Patrick Geddes. The module sought to locate the learner in their local context, and this meant incorporating studies and analysis of the local labour market, personal employment history, and the environment, in an attempt to encourage the target group to critically analyse and describe their possible career routes in their own locality.

By studying these two new modules in combination with the existing 'Study Skills' module the adult learner is being asked to think critically about themselves in the following three ways:

- as a learner (via 'Study Skills');
- as a person (via 'Individual, Family, Society: 1');
- as a citizen/employee/professional (via 'Place, Work, Folk: 1').

These modules interact closely and each seeks to produce as its main learning outcome (carrying between 50–75 per cent weighting) material that can be combined into a 'Life Learning Project' that allows the learner to discover, analyse, evaluate and choose both their future programme of study and their career aims.

All modules were validated through college academic procedures and an internal and external evaluation of the project was undertaken.

STRUCTURAL SUPPORT

The support required could be met (as far as was possible allowing for local and part-time delivery of modules) in community education sites, thus cutting transport and child-care costs for the students substantially. Funding for the students' financial needs came from a successful European Social Fund application by QMC. This will last for one year. It is hoped that the partnerships that have been developed with local communities, businesses and local government in the pilot phase will then develop into coalitions that can access longer term funding.

PERSONAL SUPPORT

This involved the development of an internal student tutor/mentor programme using final-year QMC students through the QMC student association, who came from similar backgrounds to the pilot programme students. British Petroleum International were interested in this development and funded the pilot programme to cover training and expenses for the students who would act as tutors/mentors to the pilot group. Seven final-year students from the combined studies programme were recruited and trained to act as informal guidance and skills support to the twelve pilot students.

RESULTS TO DATE

All the pilot students progressed into year two of their programme. The students organized, obtained sponsorship and took part in a joint-exchange study programme on the effects of globalization on the family between QMC, Edinburgh and the School of New Resources in New York City, in June and August 1996. The students continue to perform at above-average class levels in their second year and all are now looking towards completing their degrees.

CONCLUSION

The following areas of interest have been identified by both internal and external project evaluators:

Student response

Pilot programme students have expressed appreciation of the integrated approach of the programme and the clear progressional development from community education programmes into higher education and other active learning opportunities, such as placements with Edinburgh City Museums, as part of their level 1 programme.

Academic staff response

The response of academic staff to both the group and the programme has been very favourable. All staff involved in the project have noted that this group are among the most highly motivated group they have taught.

Points of generic interest to the higher education sector

Since the programme is still in its formative stages, it is difficult to draw conclusions but there are indications that:

- this mode of delivery appeals to/helps form a highly motivated student;
- students show a lively response to a participatory learning environment;
- effective provision for this target group need not be expensive in structural support terms if higher education institutions are prepared to become partners in educational progression in a community;

- articulation of course material and teaching approaches is possible even in educational sectors with superficially such dramatically different populations in age, social class and educational experience such as higher education and community education;
- a holistic learner-centred programme is highly rewarding for both students and staff;
- there are other funding possibilities available for this target group of students that the institutions can access;
- access to higher education can be variable in its approach and should not be seen through the lens of 'access courses'.

REFERENCES

Cross, K (1986) *Adults as Learners: Increasing Participation and Facilitating Learning*, Jossey Bass Inc., San Francisco

McGivney, V (1990) 'Education's For Other People' *Access To Particiapation for Non-Participant Adults*, NIACE, Leicester

Chapter 19

But This Isn't How an English Class is Supposed to be...

William Macauley and Gian Pagnucci

We teach first year composition at Indiana University of Pennsylvania (IUP), a public university with an enrolment of 14,000 students. Most students come from the surrounding rural region. This area is economically challenged from the drastic decline of steel and other industries over the last 20 years. The students are primarily white, working class, first-generation college students. Another large portion of the student body comes from Pittsburgh and Philadelphia. These students are more frequently African-American, also from working class backgrounds.

THE PROBLEM

Although these students have diverse backgrounds, they share common goals. College is a financial burden for poor families; these students want to know that all their college work directly relates to a profitable professional career in the near future. This creates two problems: first, students do not always see courses as valuable for their career. Second, many courses assume it is the students' job to make connections between what they are learning now and what they will need to know later.

These problems require flexibility, especially in general courses like composition. On the one hand, classes need to be more flexible so that they are adaptable to the career goals of students. On the other hand, students need the opportunity to learn flexibility so they can adapt what they learn to their goals.

A SOLUTION

A composition course might ideally be a place to develop students' skills at negotiating writing tasks. The focus on negotiating tasks rather than learning particular forms, makes the composition class more flexible. It forces students to examine a variety of documents serving diverse audiences and purposes. By focusing on negotiation, students learn to think of writing as making choices about topic, form, and audience. In learning to negotiate that process, students are better able to adapt what they learn in composition to their career needs, thus becoming more flexible learners.

In the Autumn of 1996 we designed such a course, one built around the idea of negotiating writing tasks. We worked with four sections of 'English 101: College Writing', the IUP introductory composition course. The students started by critiquing professional publications. We asked them to identify what they liked or found useful and to figure out what made those documents appealing. Students evaluated these publications based on both their textual and visual elements.

Based upon their critiques, students wrote proposals for publications they would like to create. Each student wrote three letters of application to individual project proposers. A series of e-mail letters were then sent. At the end of the application process, each student was part of two publication teams. Many of these teams cut across class sections.

Students were taught to use desktop publishing to produce professional looking publications. They spent several weeks working on these publications. Each team member was required to produce one or more articles for each publication. Most teams had a manager (normally the publication proposer) who supervised other meetings, set schedules, and reported to the instructors.

Team members could be responsible for layout, editing, graphics, and monitoring production costs. Some teams divided up tasks while other teams did all the work collaboratively. All teams were allowed flexibility to choose how they would act on the original proposal, distribute the work, and what the final publication would look like.

Along with two publications, each student was also required to complete a World Wide Web page. Students were introduced to this project and the technology necessary to complete it shortly after their publication teams had begun working. The web page work mirrored the publication process in that students began by critiquing, then proposing, and constructing their own web page.

Students were encouraged to think of class time as work time. This was based upon a studio model (Blume, 1982; Grant and Manuel, 1995;

Kaupinnen, 1987; Platt, 1991). It was emphasized that class time would be insufficient to successfully complete the course. Students were allowed flexibility in terms of which section to attend, what work to do during class time, and how to prioritize that work. For instance, students could choose to use class time to research their topics in the library or on the Internet, edit drafts, or produce layout models for their publications. Several weeks before the semester's end, students handed in their team publications. These were made available in the library. Students were then asked to evaluate the publications and the web sites. Finally, students compiled all their work into personal portfolios which included a reflective evaluation of the quality of their work during the semester.

METHODOLOGY

To assess the effects of these course changes, we followed the model of Lincoln and Guba (1985), triangulating our data by looking at student publications and web pages (the collection and use of artifacts in qualitative research is supported by Glesne and Peshkin, 1992), our teaching journals (as supported by Hollingsworth, 1994), and course evaluations (Bernard, 1995). These data represented three distinct sources of information: student work, teachers' observations and experiences, and student observations and evaluation.

We were trying to generate an impressionistic description of what we and our students experienced rather than quantifiable data regarding each of the individual changes we made. This approach is in line with a narrative inquiry model (Connelly and Clandinin 1990; Pagnucci and Abt-Perkins 1992; Schaafsma 1993).

Our data analysis began with discussing our personal impressions of our own composition sections. We then compared those impressions to develop a common understanding of how these new teaching methods had changed the course. Then we looked for specific evidence, of these changes within our three data sources. Using specific evidence, or the lack of it, we were able to generate some conclusions about the value of this new pedagogical approach.

OUTCOMES

Our teacher journals indicated a drastic change in the character of our classes. In the past, our classes were full of students who slouched in the back of the room, looked bored, and waited for us to perform our teaching. Sometimes they listened, sometimes they slept. We ran the class, and they did what we told them to do. We moved through classes like wading through mud, and the measure of success was usually endurance.

After their redesign, our courses were full of students who raced around the room collecting printouts, checking information on the web, and seeking advice. They would not wait for us. They depended on each other, ran their teams, and told us what they needed. The class became a swirl of movement, sound, and energy. They had their own ideals for their projects, and measured success by their progress toward those visions. They worked to meet their own goals, not ours. We worked to help them solve real problems.

The students worked harder than we ever expected. Their publications were innovative and included a fashion guidebook, a children's geography book, a student cookbook, as well as Internet sites ranging from abstract art to the X-Files. Each student's letters, critiques, articles, evaluations, reports, and technology user guides totalled 22 different assignments by the end of the semester, and over 80 pages of material for their portfolios. We found publications and web pages that were well written, substantially developed, and creative. These documents demonstrated an awareness of audience, skill at working in different genres, expertise at visually representing information, and a high degree of coherence.

The publication prefaces were rich information sources. Many students discussed overcoming team conflicts, struggling to meet deadlines, and learning how to accomplish the goals they had set for themselves. They saw clear evidence of improvement in writing, teamwork, time management, leadership, and organizational skills. They also expressed deep pride in their publications. The volume, variety, and quality of the work our students produced was evidence to us that the flexibility of our course encouraged the same in our students.

A final source of data, the student evaluations, helped demonstrate the success of our new course design. Ninety per cent of our students said this course was more or much more work than other courses of equal credit value. Eighty-five per cent said that what they learned in the course was valuable. Eighty-five per cent said they would recommend the course to a friend.

CONCLUSION

We drew several conclusions from our data:

- Our new course was a much more active learning environment because of the level of activity and engagement we saw in our students.

- Students were given the opportunity to negotiate writing tasks and they did it well. This is supported by the quality of the student publications and web sites.

- Students are able to find value in work when they can turn it to their own purposes. This is evident in the evaluations since students recommended the course despite thinking it was more work.

This case study demonstrates that, in this context, flexibility has improved the quality of our students work. Learners were active, engaged, and eager to write. The data is limited and subjective, but we believe this research is a useful first step toward uncovering specific links between flexibility and the reflective teaching of writing.

REFERENCES

Bernard, H R (1995) *Research Methods in Anthropology: Qualitative and Quantitative Methods,*(2nd edn) AltaMira, Walnut Creek, California

Blume, S (1982) 'Drawing at the Albright-Knox Gallery' *School Arts*, 81 (8) pp. 30–3

Connelly, F M and Clandinin, D J (1990)'Stories of experience and narrative inquiry' *Educational Researcher*, 19 (5) pp. 2–14

Glesne, C and Peshkin, A (1992) *Becoming Qualitative Researchers: An Introduction*, Longman, New York

Grant, J and Manuel, P (1995) 'Using a peer resource learning-model in planning education' *Journal of Planning Education and Research*, 15 (1) pp. 51–7

Hollingsworth, S (1994) *Teacher Research and Urban Literacy Education: Lessons and Conversations in a Feminist Key*, Teachers College, New York

Kaupinnen, H (1987) 'Teaching about architecture' *Art Education*, 40 (1) pp. 44–9

Lincoln, Y S and Guba, E G (1985) *Naturalistic Inquiry*, Sage, Newbury Park

Pagnucci, G and Abt-Perkins, D (1992) 'The never making sense story: Reassessing the value of narrative' *English Journal*, 81, pp. 54–8

Platt, H (1991) 'Creating a writing studio', *Writing Notebook: Creative Wordprocessing in the Classroom*, 9 (2) pp. 7–9, 14

Schaafsma, D (1993) *Eating on the Street: Teaching Literacy in a Multicultural Society*, University of Pittsburgh, Pittsburgh

Chapter 20

Student SkillPacks

Rosie Bingham and Sue Drew

This chapter describes a project to produce materials to help students develop those skills often called 'transferable' or 'key'. When the project began in 1993, the importance of encouraging students' skill development was generally accepted in Sheffield Hallam University.

The impetus for the project was a request for support by tutors delivering a personal and professional development unit in the School of Engineering. TEED (now the Department for Education and Employment) provided funding of £30,000 for a SkillPacks project which would develop materials to cater for all students from all disciplines, and which could be integrated within subjects. The project was based in the University's Learning and Teaching Institute, which supports staff in educational development.

Semesterization, modularization and reducing resources have resulted in increasing pressure on class time, so that the materials needed to be used by students independently as well as in class. The ready-made materials would save academic staff time, and would provide support where staff felt lacking in expertise to meet widening student skill needs. They would focus on self-awareness and reflection, rather than being prescriptive.

THE PROJECT METHODOLOGY

The following titles of SkillPacks were identified through consultation with staff and students.

Skills directly relevant to course activities	Underpinning skills
Group Work	Identifying Strengths
Solving Problems	Improving Skills
Gathering and Using Information	Organizing Yourself and Your Time
Report Writing	
Revising and Examination Techniques	Coping With Pressure
	Negotiating and Assertiveness
Oral Presentation	Confidence with Numbers*
Note-taking	Reflecting on Experience*
Essay Writing*	
IT SkillPacks – a further series*	*added after the TEED funded project

A SkillPack for each topic was drafted, using literature searches, exploring other further education and higher education materials and practice, and with extensive consultation with academic staff.

A thorough and extensive evaluation of the materials was a key feature of the project, a vital part of the development process. A range of qualitative and quantitative data were collected from 2800 staff and students, using the following methods, each offering different benefits.

- Structured group sessions with students. Students were asked what they liked and disliked about the SkillPack and what aspects of the skill they needed most help with. These results gave specific ideas on improving the individual packs and on further needs.

- A questionnaire reached more students, provided quantitative data, and enabled analysis against the following variables – age, ethnic origin, gender, route into higher education, entry qualification and student perceptions of their skill expertise (due to variation in assessment practice, data on assessed skill performance could not be collected). The open-ended questions produced further qualitative data.

- Staff and students were observed using the SkillPacks, covering a range of disciplines and class sizes. This gave ideas about the ways in which the Packs could be used and the differing teaching techniques employed. This subsequently formed part of the 'Tutor Notes' which offer guidance on how to use the Packs effectively.

MAIN FINDINGS

Skill improvement

More than half the respondents rated their current expertise negatively. Seventy-six per cent of respondents rated their skill as having improved after using the SkillPacks positively, with 22–24 year olds (those who had rated their current skill level as 'poor') and male students rating their skill improvement the greatest.

Content, format and language

The overall view was very positive, even where students felt they already knew some of the information. Suggestions were seen as appropriate, the examples helpful, and students commonly found the SkillPacks raised their awareness. The variation in student responses to the materials led to development and production at two levels.

Ninety-six per cent of students liked the overall structure and format, which made the SkillPacks clear and easy to use, although some were too long. The students responded positively to the SkillPack being printed on different coloured paper for each skill. There was a mixed response to the self-completion boxes and action plans, with many students feeling that while these were helpful, there were too many. It was very important that the language was not patronizing.

Usage

The SkillPacks were most successfully used:

- where students acknowledged the need for them at a particular stage in their course, eg for an assignment;
- where they were given at an appropriate time, eg 'Oral Presentation' given three weeks before a presentation, 'Negotiating and Assertiveness' given in relation to a placement;
- where the skill was assessed and clear criteria were given. Some SkillPacks were used for self-assessment and personal action planning and students were required to make a personal statement in relation to the skill;
- where they were used in conjunction with other SkillPacks, eg 'Group Work' with 'Negotiating and Assertiveness';
- either in class sessions with a set task, or for discussion;

- where tutors placed the SkillPack in context so students appreciated the value of the skill; organized the sessions effectively; participated in the discussion; and gave clear information about assignments and criteria.

Student preferences

- 'Group Work', 'Oral Presentation', 'Report Writing', 'Note-Taking' and 'Solving Problems' were the SkillPacks most in demand.

- The educational/employment background, age, and gender of students influences their perception of materials. This implies tutors need to allow for students in any one class having differing views on the relevance of a SkillPack.

- Mature students (22–35 years plus) do perceive a need for skill development and are not less interested in it than younger students.

- Mature students are more likely to perceive the need for underpinning skills. This suggests the need for increasing awareness in younger students.

- Students coming from school are less likely to recognize the importance of professional rather than academic skills.

- Traditional study skills are perceived as being most needed by those with the least recent experience of academia.

- The most popular SkillPacks among women were those relating to personal, interpersonal and communication skills. This may indicate differences in values influencing how men and women respond to teaching and assessment activities.

KEY FEATURES OF THE FINAL VERSIONS OF THE SKILL-PACKS

- The SkillPacks are designed to be used across disciplines. The examples used are multi-disciplinary but tutors can add their own.

- The SkillPacks can either be used in class or as stand-alone handouts.

- Each skill has SkillPacks at two levels. The learning outcomes are based on National Council for Vocational Qualification (NCVQ) Core Skill levels 3 and 4, are given in each SkillPack, and can be used as criteria for self- or tutor-assessment.

- The SkillPacks are based on raising self-awareness and are not prescriptive.
- There is an individual SkillPack for each skill area, designed for use with a specific task.
- A SkillPack can be used in conjunction with other SkillPacks.
- They are relevant, concise, colourful, and structured.
- The language is not patronizing.
- They are very flexible.

WHAT IS HAPPENING NOW?

Indications are that the SkillPacks do what was intended and they have been much in demand. Logistical issues seem the only threat to their usage.

- In a modular system how can you avoid duplication between units and ensure progression in skill development between levels/years?
- Where is the time for skills work in a semesterized system with 12 weeks teaching for a unit?
- How can a distribution and payment system be established in a decentralized institution?
- How can schools square using the SkillPacks with a requirement to reduce photocopying budgets?
- Given these issues, how can the SkillPacks be used as the evaluation suggested, in conjunction with a task, at an appropriate time, with tutor support, and with assessment?

Our solutions have included: lodging originals with the print unit from where schools order and pay for copies; an administrative contact in each school; coordination of usage through programme or course leaders; library reference sets; distributing brief tutor notes to all university staff.

EXAMPLES OF USAGE

In virtually all Sheffield Hallam University schools there is a level 1 skills unit and, although the orientation differs in each school, all attempt to ensure relevance to the rest of the course. Examples include the School of Science and Maths where 330 students, in small groups, develop scientific kits. They are assessed via a poster, report and oral presentation, and a portfolio presenting evidence of their skills. Workshops support the skills needed and four SkillPacks are used. The SkillPacks are also used in other units and at other levels: 'Group Work' helps students in a housing studies level 2 unit which consists totally of a group project; education students have submitted completed parts of the SkillPacks as evidence of teaching competences.

The SkillPacks have attracted interest nationally and internationally and have been published as books for tutors and students and as photocopiable originals (Drew and Bingham 1996; 1997). A small grant has been obtained from the Department of Education and Employment to turn 'Oral Presentation' into an interactive computer package, and there is interest in Sheffield Hallam University in using SkillPacks for the increasing number of postgraduate distance learning programmes. We are trialling information technology (IT) SkillPacks. Students who come to Sheffield Hallam University with a wide range of existing IT skills, can use a self-diagnosis guide to identify which level IT SkillPack they need and in what topic, and whether their needs are best met by the Packs or by the University's other documents about particular packages.

Nationally there is continuing focus on core/key skills, with the Dearing review of 16–19 year olds' qualifications (1996), the current Dearing review of higher education, and the debate on graduateness engendered by the Higher Education Quality Council (HEQC, 1996). Although the titles are context-specific to higher education, the SkillPacks fall into the full range of core/key skills specified by Oates (NCVQ, 1992) and can be used to support core/key skill development in advanced General National Vocational Qualifications or for the core/key skill units separately accredited by the Royal Society of Arts, and BTEC (Business and Technician Education Council).

CONCLUSION

The project was unusual in the extent to which the materials were evaluated, providing guidance on content, format and usage. The SkillPacks are very flexible, can be used by a wide range of students from all disciplines, and can be stand-alone or used in class. Their learning outcomes can help in identifying assessment criteria, and the two levels meet the needs of individual students' different starting points and of different course requirements. They are cost effective, compact, to the point, and easy to follow. They have proved a popular contribution to overcoming the problems of how to support students and staff in integrating skill development with their subjects.

REFERENCES

Dearing, R (1996) *Review of qualifications for 16–19 year olds*, School Curriculum and Assessment Authority, Hayes, Middlesex

Drew, S and Bingham, R (1996) *Students Skills. Tutor's Handbook*, Gower, Aldershot

Drew, S and Bingham, R (1997) *The Students Skills Guide*, Gower, Aldershot

Drew, S and Bingham, R (1997) *Student Skills SkillPack Masters*, Gower, Aldershot

HEQC Quality Enhancement Group (1996) *A paper to stimulate discussion. What are graduates? Clarifying the attributes of 'graduateness'* HEQC, London

Oates, T (1992) *Developing and piloting the NCVQ core skill units. An outline of method and summary of findings. Report 16*, NCVQ, London

Chapter 21

An Interactive Library Skills Workbook for Engineering Undergraduates

Clare Bainbridge

This study describes an interactive, library skills workbook used at the University of the West of England, Bristol. Those using the book are approximately 290 first-year undergraduates and Higher National Diploma (HND) students on full-time courses, studying for qualifications in electrical, mechanical, aeronautical or manufacturing engineering in the Faculty of Engineering.

INTRODUCTION

Target students for this exercise are first-year undergraduate and HND students in engineering. In previous years they have been offered as library sessions, but these have been poorly marketed, and timetabled in such a way as to make attendance unlikely. The sessions were not related to the students' assignments, so very few people attended. The students are mostly campus-based, with a few visiting from further education (FE) colleges where they are attending franchised courses.

My aims in developing the workbook were four-fold:

- to provide library skills education in a form students would actually use;
- to take students through the logical process of a literature search rather than demonstrating resources in a relatively unstructured way;
- to familiarize students with the library;
- to encourage students to think critically about information sources.

The rationale for choosing a flexible learning approach was that two of the key objectives were to encourage critical thinking and to enable the students to use the library confidently. A workbook enabled these objectives to be met. The same material might have been incorporated into an interactive computer-based resource, but that would have denied students the chance to familiarize themselves with the actual physical nature (and location) of the paper-based materials they will still largely be required to use in their work. Demonstrations in a seminar group of around 20 are not conducive to active learning, while a practical exercise asking the right questions might hopefully elicit a more critical approach.

Since we do not see the students again, there is no chance of giving or gaining feedback, unless it can be built into the book. Therefore the workbook is designed to provide feedback at each stage. It also allows students to work at their own pace. Students who are having difficulty completing it within three hours are encouraged to come and ask for extra help.

THE DEVELOPMENT STAGE

At the planning stage, meetings were held with the member of staff responsible for modules in professional and communications skills within the Faculty of Engineering.

I found that I already had a considerable amount of material, such as exercises previously used with students, which only needed adapting to fit the new requirements. I teach the students for three one-hour sessions, which counts as part of the module. I am available for consultation during each of those sessions, but attendance is only compulsory at the first one, at which the books are given out and the purpose of the exercise explained. Books are handed in a week after the last session and marked by me before being returned to the students. Marks take 15 per cent of the module total. In 1995 the workbook was completed by 172 students out of a possible 293.

The workbook has cost little more than the various handouts which preceded it, and this was an important consideration in choosing this model, though by no means a deciding one.

DESIGN AND STRUCTURE

The workbook is divided into sections, in imitation of the stages of the literature search. The topic of the search is 'engineering design'. This seemed to be the only example which would be relevant to students studying the various different branches of engineering. Previous experience suggests that engineering students are particularly reluctant to engage in exercises of doubtful relevance.

The opening section demonstrates the method used throughout the book, and asks students to cite some of the aims and objectives of the exercise and to think about the advantages and disadvantages of working in the timetabled sessions or on their own.

Subsequent sections ask students to think about keywords and how they can be used to broaden or narrow a search; how to make best use of reference materials; and how to locate, access and use abstracts and indexes in hard copy and on CD-ROM databases. Students are finally given a single reference, as it comes from a database, and asked to use the guidelines in the workbook to cite it in a style acceptable to the faculty. These sample references are printed from the INSPEC CD-ROM database of electronic and computing material, largely because that comes in a complex format which the students often find difficult to understand.

Each section opens with a brief description of the material it covers. Practical exercises follow, with questions which begin with the factual (how many references are there?) and move on to concepts the students find more challenging (why does it matter how many references there are?). Each section closes with feedback suggesting various possible answers or hints as to how the questions might have been approached.

ADVANTAGES OF THE WORKBOOK APPROACH

The workbook allows students to work at their own pace. They can also choose whether to work alone or in small groups. For those lacking in confidence the possibility of working with a more assertive partner can be beneficial, and this also seems to enable students whose first language is not English to get peer group help. It enables students to work in ways and times that suit them. It allows the librarian to spend time actively supporting students who are already engaged in a learning task, rather than talking to groups where there may be little active engagement by the learners.

SOME DISADVANTAGES

There are three possible drawbacks to the use of the workbook. First, it is quite possible for students to evade the work in the book, either by copying from others or by simply being prepared to forego the marks for the exercise. However, compared to the very small numbers participating in library skills education previously, completion rates for the book are very high. Second, self-directed learning can feel challenging to the students, and there is the possibility that students who find it hard to cope but who are not willing to identify themselves as needing extra help may simply fall through the net. Third, a workbook can only cover a very small proportion of the types of information resources available. Searching for standards or patents, for example, is not covered, though their existence is noted.

CONCLUSION

At the end of the workbook is an evaluation sheet, which was filled in by 165 of the 172 students completing the task:

- 82 found the work quite easy, 71 quite hard;
- 109 had 'enough time' to complete it, 34 had 'not enough time' and 21 had 'too much time';
- 101 found the tone 'helpful' or 'friendly', 25 said it was 'patronizing' and 8 'too technical'.

The most satisfactory feedback was that 101 students said that the exercise made them feel 'more comfortable' in the library, though 54 said it made 'no difference'. There seemed to be no correlation between those who said they found the work hard and those obtaining low marks. It will be difficult to be certain about the effectiveness of the workbook until students come through to the final year, when the requirement to undertake a major project often exposes lack of information-retrieval and information-handling skills.

As far as it is possible to say at this stage, this exercise in introducing a flexible learning approach has been reasonably successful. More students are taking part in information skills education, and their participation is of a more active nature. It is worrying, though, that nearly half the students are still not taking part, even though this figure is a considerable improvement on the 5 per cent previous attendance level. Those who fail to do so can, of course, be given the workbook at the stage where they become aware of needing information skills. Another concern is that the implementation of the workbook has been entirely dependent on the interest and goodwill of a member of teaching staff, and unless the position can be formalized in some way, it will continue to be so.

My intention is to move this initiative on, first by redesigning the workbook in a way which makes it more challenging intellectually (it is still very much under development) and ultimately by using an open, critical thinking approach such as that described by Atton (1994) on using critical thinking in library education, which seems to me to pursue the advantages of student-directed learning to its logical conclusion.

REFERENCES

Atton, C (1994) 'Using critical thinking as a basis for library user education' *Journal of Academic Librarianship*, 20 (5/6) November, pp. 310–313

Chapter 22

Introducing Computer Networks as a Research Tool to First-Year Postgraduates

Richard Steward

This course was aimed at ensuring that all new postgraduates in Animal and Microbial Sciences (AMS) at the University of Reading were introduced to the facilities available to support research on the campus network. In many areas of biomedical research, the ability to locate and manipulate information via the Internet (such as DNA sequences) is an essential research skill. These skills can also be viewed as transferable skills which would help postgraduates when they come into contact with science-based industry, either during or after their postgraduate studies.

INTRODUCTION

The course came about because of an initiative within the AMS Department to revise the introductory courses for new postgraduates. The main investment for the course was provided by the department, which set up ten new computers connected to the campus network, in a room available to the postgraduates.

The new course for postgraduates offered the opportunity to apply some of the teaching approaches developed during the BIONET Teaching and Learning Technology Project programme for biology undergraduates and teaching graduates in the computer industry.

A number of special considerations relevant to the target group indicated the need for a flexible approach:

* The research topics vary widely, ranging from zoology to the study of viruses and disease.

- Postgraduates in their first year often feel under pressure to meet target dates for developing their methods, and producing initial progress reports. Consequently, other commitments have to be fitted in and around their main concerns.

- Some participants will already have a good grasp of the facilities available. Others may be at a disadvantage if they are uncertain how to access the facilities available, and lack any appreciation of the potential benefits for their research.

AIMS FOR THE COURSE

The general aim for the first running of the course was to provide all new postgraduates with an appreciation of some of the computing facilities available to support research on the University of Reading network.

The specific aims were that:

- For some participants, the topics would be of immediate relevance.

- For others, the course manual would help them recognize opportunities for applying some of the ideas at a later stage of their project.

- All participants would be briefed in some of the 'industry-standard' approaches to information-handling which have become dominant in organizations employing biologists at postgraduate level.

PLANNING FOR THE COURSE

The software already available on the University of Reading campus was examined during July 1995. The software was compared against the following list of requirements for the postgraduate course:

- The aim would be to keep the course within a consistent software environment by using just one or two multi-purpose packages. If two packages are used then there should be some obvious split of functions, eg one is used for entering data and one is used for analysing data. There should be an easy link between the two systems.

- The statistical software should combine an ability to give novice users confidence that they can produce results quickly with enough potential power to cope with more rigorous data analysis requirements.

- It would be desirable to provide for *ad hoc* data analysis. Comparisons with the more formal statistical tests included should suggest some of the advantages and limitations of new approaches to examining sets of data (sometimes called data mining).

- If possible, the software included should be used widely by biologists in research and laboratory organizations. An appreciation of the software should therefore be a contribution to the transferable skills acquired by participants.

The conclusion was that two existing packages – SAS (SAS Software Limited) and ORACLE (Oracle Corporation UK Ltd) – could be integrated to illustrate a number of capabilities relevant to research:

- data analysis;
- report writing and presentation;
- data simulation;
- multivariate statistics;
- data mining.

SAS is a very powerful statistics package which can be used to produce tables, charts and graphs to support the production of reports. It includes an introductory module called SAS/ASSIST.

ORACLE is software which allows a user to define a database, put data in the database and query back the data in a very flexible way. The commands used to do these are relatively simple to learn and the language used (structured query language (SQL)) is common to a whole range of database products produced by different companies.

APPROACH ADOPTED

The training was designed to fit in with the complex time demands of postgraduate research. It was therefore decided to base it around a comprehensive manual. This was aimed at giving enough background information to allow participants to work through the demonstrations at their own pace. In addition, the manual should be helpful if retained as a reference for participants whose requirements for data analysis only emerge during the second or third years of their study.

It was decided to include in the manual a glossary of all technical terms which were used. The manual would also include examples of the type of output which should be seen when the demonstrations were run on a computer.

A 60-page manual was developed which was designed to be flexible. It would not be necessary to work through the whole material during a single session. The initial part of the manual would give an introduction to the statistics/data presentation package (SAS). The remainder would introduce the database (ORACLE) for storing and retrieving data and producing simple simulations.

It was assumed that some participants would have a low priority for topics not of immediate relevance to their research. For these participants, a short introductory session would probably be sufficient for their immediate requirements, with the manual being retained for reference.

INTRODUCTORY SESSION

A trial session with a draft of the manual was made with the cooperation of two AMS postgraduates in October 1995. This was valuable in further refining the approach. For example, it was decided to provide two pages of hints based on all the occasions on which the course author had been forced to work out a solution. This was in the form of a 'frequently asked questions' section.

Drawing on experience from designing courses in the computer industry, it was decided to try to ensure that everyone had an initial introductory session. This was to overcome any barriers to using the manual. For example, there were slight differences between the 'computer environment' which the participants worked in, when they accessed the network by their 'username' and 'password accounts'. This meant one of the initial instructions had to be slightly altered for some of the participants.

The only prerequisite for the introductory session was that each participant be given a username and password by the computer services department. Times were allocated for each student to have their introductory session on a one-to-one basis. Communication by electronic mail was used to rearrange dates to suit individuals as required. The introductory session generally took about one hour per participant. Electronic mail was also used to put one participant in touch with someone with specific experience in the type of data analysis involved in their research project.

The manual was circulated to 20 postgraduates. Thirteen introductory sessions were run. By April 1996, only one person who had expressed a definite interest in having an initial introduction had still failed to appear.

CONCLUSION

To assess the extent to which the aims had been achieved, a questionnaire was circulated to all the participants by electronic mail. Ten responses were received before the end of the study. All had received the manual and thought it contained adequate background material (although one person wanted more information about file transfer).

The replies indicated that, as would be expected from the diversity of research interests, less than half of the students would be applying things learnt directly to their research. The replies indicated that all the ORACLE software was new to all of the participants. The SAS software had only been previously encountered by two participants.

The course seems to have made efficient use of the available resources (ie one person part-time). It could be argued that running the course in the second year of a PhD course would ensure that the participants had a greater motivation to master issues of data analysis and handling. However, preparing the students in the initial year, when research strategies are being formulated, may have a more beneficial pay-off at a later stage of a research project.

SAS and ORACLE are likely to remain highly relevant for the next five years at least. No urgent need for revision of the manual has been identified and the course is being repeated in 1997. The performance of postgraduates is obviously vital for the future well-being of the department. This course seems to particularly benefit the proportion of new postgraduates who would otherwise experience barriers to making use of the computer network as a valuable resource.

SECTION IV
Institutional Strategies for Supporting Flexible Learning

INTRODUCTION

Sections I to III have focused on a range of small-scale independent flexible learning initiatives. This section is distinct in that its focus is on institution and department-wide policies and strategies developed to facilitate flexible learning. The case studies present a selection of organizational approaches to the provision of increased flexibility, at a time when many in higher education are reviewing their policies on teaching and learning in response to the drivers mentioned in the introduction to this book.

Only a few of the case studies provide a clear view of the pedagogic basis which underlies the successful exploitation of flexible learning. The rationales discussed in several of the case studies in this section echo those of the smaller-scale initiatives encountered earlier in the book. The recurring themes have been access, student choice, appropriate student support and maintaining quality at a time of resource constraint. They illustrate the wide range of current concerns and approaches to providing increased flexibility.

William Lynch (Chapter 23) opens this section with a case study from George Washington University, United States of America, and some challenging questions about the future of higher education and the role of the traditional university. This is one of several case studies to emphasize the need for an appropriate infrastructure, management and support systems for both students and staff. Stephen Fallows (Chapter 24) also addresses this in his discussion of the underlying managerial and pedagogic rationale for the adoption of a 'mixed mode' model for undergraduate course delivery at Luton University, England. Sally Anderson (Chapter 30) presents an account of policy development and implementation relating to the introduction of flexible learning at Napier University, Scotland.

Many of the cases in this book describe and evaluate the adoption of new course delivery methods using new technologies. Cathy Hole (Chapter 28) recounts experiences at Bristol University, England, in establishing an open learning centre as part of the institution-wide information technology learning strategy. The problems and successes of the pilot project are evaluated in the light of converging technologies and the potential for electronic delivery of learning resources campus wide. Philip Barker (Chapter 27) describes an electronic Open Access Student Information Service (OASIS) at the University of Teesside, England, to provide local and remote students with flexible access to electronic lecture material and other learning resources. (See also Fulkerth (Chapter 1), where his individual initiative in online course delivery is likely to form part of an institution-wide development, the Cybercampus.)

Patrick McGhee (Chapter 26) reviews the experiences of a new psychology department committed to student-centred flexible learning at the University of Derby, England. He identifies the benefits of adopting an integrationist strategy to course delivery and learning resources, and discusses approaches developed to address problems associated with the shift to flexible provision. The uses of video technology to deliver courses and meet student needs is also described.

Many of the issues confronting higher education transcend national boundaries. For example, Tony Cavanagh's case from Deakin University, Australia (Chapter 25), demonstrates the international parallels confronting librarians today in determining the library's role in supporting flexible learning.

Although many case studies have mentioned the changing role for lecturers implied in a shift towards more flexible learning, the case study from Stockport College, England, written by Jackie Robinson (Chapter 29) is the only one to focus specifically on the need for staff development to ensure that both tutorial and support staff are equipped with appropriate skills to support flexible learners.

The institutional and departmental strategies in this chapter also detail processes that have been adopted to develop learning skills to improve the quality of the student learning experience. Winnie Wade (Chapter 31) concludes this section with a description of the initiative at Loughborough University, England, designed to support the development of students' learning skills. This case study details the integration of learning skills into subject curricula and an evaluation of aspects essential for success (see also Bingham and Drew, Chapter 20).

Chapter 23

Flexible Learning: Is it as Good for the University as it is for the Students?

William Lynch

The Educational Technology Leadership (ETL) programme is currently the only programme of its kind distributed entirely at a distance, and is the largest distance programme at the George Washington University. It was created to provide flexible access to quality higher education for individuals whose geographic location, job requirements, schedule, or family responsibilities made traditional campus-based study unfeasible or undesirable. Most of the ETL students have full-time jobs as teachers, educational administrators, media coordinators, instructional media developers, or are training specialists in schools, business, or government-sponsored organizations. Offered using a combination of asynchronous and synchronous communications, the programme provides the opportunity for extensive interaction with fellow students and faculty via computer networks, and a chance to share learning experiences with other educational professionals around the world.

THE PROBLEM

Flexible approaches to learning, including distance education, are unquestionably advantageous and beneficial to students. Education is acquired in a more accommodating fashion, typically at a lower cost, and often with greater attention to the students' needs. Is this market-sensitive approach to teaching and learning good for the University? How will the provision of flexible learning structures and validation mechanisms affect universities and colleges in the future? These are two of the most important questions emerging from our current experiences in higher educational evolution.

As knowledge is increasingly commodified amid predictions that workers will need to re-educate themselves with increased frequency, traditional institutions of higher education are slowly losing their monopoly on the knowledge distribution industry. In the twenty-first century, convenience and effectiveness will be the benchmarks of successful educational programmes. Educational providers that survive market forces will either provide very high quality education or provide it at great convenience. The best educational providers will do both. Some institutions of higher education understand this reality explicitly, others are reluctantly exploring their options. Universities however, are by tradition, culture, and policy poorly designed to become what is now popularly called the virtual university. The success or failure of distance education at a specific institution is predicated on the ability of the institution's systems to accommodate the needs and desires of non-traditional, non-resident students.

Examining characteristics of the ETL programme may provide some insight into the future of the university of the next century. To pursue this end, four areas of traditional university practices, and virtual university requirements, will be examined. The four areas covered will be: curriculum development and production; instruction; technical support; and administrative support.

CURRICULUM DEVELOPMENT AND PRODUCTION

The basic design of a curriculum may be outlined in programme goals or a general curriculum plan, but the specifics that are embedded in courses and other experiences are typically designed by the lecturers who will be responsible for instruction. In a traditional university instructional environment, lecturers determine what is to be taught and most often use basic technologies for communication. The time required for preparation is built into a lecturer's workload, especially if the course has been taught before. University personnel understand the amount of time required to prepare for a traditional class. In the flexible learning environment of the ETL programme, additional time must be spent planning, organizing resources, coordinating activities, preparing materials, and scheduling production cycles. Even if the instruction is offered live, it should appear better planned than traditional instruction. Consequently, students and staff are involved collaboratively in learning, not as a transfer of information, but as a creative process. It is important to recognize that the difference in the job requoteuirements lies outside the basic concept of a lecturer's role and workload structure as defined by the university.

INSTRUCTION

The second area to be examined is instruction. Instruction in a flexible learning environment can be conceptually separated from curriculum development and production. It is possible, and perhaps desirable, that curriculum development be accomplished by a team which may or may not include the instructor or course deliverer. By separating these tasks greater efficiency and economy can be achieved, but the traditional lecturer's role is altered dramatically. Instruction for the ETL programme is defined as the relationship established with students to facilitate learning. The instructor adds value to designed learning experiences, explains conceptual nuances, stimulates creative and collaborative thinking, evaluates student performance, and makes curricular adjustments as necessary. In large groups, the instructor also coordinates co-instructors who work with smaller sections of students. Students contribute interactively to the instructional process by offering constructive criticism and feedback. The instructional process is a dynamic and flexible one which could not be easily accommodated within traditional structures.

TECHNICAL SUPPORT

The third area of interest is technical support. The method by which students connect with the virtual university and its professors and related staff is inherently technical. The need for technical support, therefore, is self-evident. In the ETL programme everything from tape delivery to cable access and web-links to file sharing implies a potential need for technical support. The traditional university has corresponding technical support roles in the context of the library, computer centre, physical plant access, and so on. The importance of technical support cannot be overstated. Successful distance students must be adept with the tools of communication; technical support staff continually assess competence, coordinate individual skill development, and work to improve the communications system. Support structures for students can become enormously expensive and demand for these services can become unmanageable. ETL students have developed peer support strategies which complement the programme initiatives, again supporting real needs in flexible time.

ADMINISTRATIVE SUPPORT

The fourth and final area of comparison is administrative support. Traditional universities are designed for traditional students, so it is not surprising that distance students are problematic for the system, with non-standard tuition rates, timetables, etc. They do not fall into the category of students who can pick up a form or sign a document or read materials distributed physically on campus. Even student policies governing residency requirements and admission deadlines fit the traditional paradigm more comfortably than a distance learning approach. The ETL programme has essentially developed a linking structure which enables articulation between the special needs of distance learners and a distance programme with the traditional university bureaucracy. The mechanics of this method are labour intensive and essentially represent special requests for system performance. The programme director and administrative coordinator continually build bridges between the needs of the distance system and the capabilities of the traditional university system.

University personnel at all levels have been eager and willing to help solve problems that occur as a result of the dissonance between the traditional systems and the needs of flexible learning. The result, however, has been the development of a parallel administrative structure to support the ETL programme. Integrating distance education support into the university needs to occur structurally, but the integration of distance learning strategies into the existing educational programme is also essential. The boundaries of traditional on-campus classes have been blurred and expanded with the use of computer-based teaching modules, online databases, and electronic mail. Each of these changes will require institutional modification. Some of the change in traditional face-to-face classes will come incrementally, but other more radical efforts are also underway.

CONCLUSION

Distance education and flexible learning as concepts are embedded with values about education, learning, and the roles that educators and learners might play in the future. These values raise fundamental questions about the role of the traditional university. As evidenced by the ETL programme, the act of implementing flexible and distance learning programmes initiates the process of addressing these questions. Universities are well known for advancing the frontiers of knowledge; it is what they are designed to do. When it comes to advancing the concept of the university itself, however, we are slow to change. Hundreds of years of tradition provide stability, but the university must also evolve if it is to survive. The danger to the university is not that it might change as a result of the flexible approaches to learning, but that it might be replaced by organizations that are more adept at meeting contemporary needs. The efforts of traditional universities to reconcile the idea of flexible learning with traditional values should be a healthy activity resulting in improvements in both campus based and distance education. It will stimulate examination of assumptions, policies and practices that will make it possible to reinvent a more useful, competitive, and vibrant university.

Chapter 24

Adopting a Mixed-Mode Approach to Teaching and Learning: A Case Study of the University of Luton

Stephen Fallows

The University of Luton is a major United Kingdom university with around 9000 full-time and a further 5000 students studying by part-time or work-based learning mode. All students are within the higher education sector. The University is also currently England's newest university, having attained this status in 1993.

The adoption of a 'mixed-mode' approach to teaching and learning has been a key element in the University's strategic development as it has contributed to each of the following:

- the expansion of student numbers;
- the increase in the range of subjects available for study;
- the diversification of opportunity for study;
- the broadening of the learning experience for its students.

The distribution of the contribution between each of the above has clearly changed over time, but the willingness of the institution to be 'flexible' in its approach has been a constant feature.

THE MIXED-MODE APPROACH

The conventional approach to higher education is campus focused and based on face-to-face activities such as lectures, seminars and tutorials.

This organization of courses, whether full- or part-time, requires students to attend predetermined locations at predetermined times. The model applies throughout higher education from the small group focus of the ancient collegiate universities to the mass access model which is common in the less well-endowed institutions. The face-to-face approach allows for student questioning and direct feedback from teacher to student. But, in addition to a concentration on the delivery of the curriculum, such an approach imposes a considerable infrastructure requirement on the institution – for instance, the provision of lecture theatres, teaching laboratories and libraries of sufficient capacity, as well as catering and student accommodation.

The opposite end of the higher education spectrum is found in the distance teaching universities of which the UK's Open University is a excellent example. Here the students and teachers are separated by both physical distance and by time (since open learning materials will be used for several years). The curriculum is largely delivered using printed resources, backed up by media such as television; direct tutor contact is limited. The distance approach avoids the structural implications of conventional higher education but requires considerable emphasis on the provision of high quality open learning materials. This model also requires a great deal of independence from its students who must display significant self-motivation, drive, and study skills. The distance model is largely targeted at adult learners; the Open University (for example) does not seek to cater for the younger student moving to higher education direct from school.

Internationally, there are some institutions, best described as 'dual-mode', in which campus-based students are taught in the conventional manner while separate programmes use distance learning methodologies for off-campus students. Often in such 'dual-mode' institutions, staff concentrate their attention on one approach with the result that there is little synergy between the two educational methodologies.

A fourth approach – the 'mixed-mode' – is being accepted by an increasing number of institutions. Here, open learning materials created primarily for distance learners are also being used by on-campus students. In most instances, the shift to the 'mixed-mode' is a strategy adopted by universities which previously were 'dual-mode' but which nowadays see benefit (educational as well as economic) in transferring their open learning materials (developed for distance learners) into the campus-based provision. However, there is an alternative 'mixed-mode' approach in which a formerly conventional university with no large-scale experience of distance learning adopts a strategy of utilizing open learning materials prepared elsewhere (for distance teaching) within its on-campus provision.

MIXED MODE AT THE UNIVERSITY OF LUTON

History

Open learning has existed at the University of Luton since the early 1980s when a centralized Open Learning Unit was established at the former Luton College of Higher Education. The Unit sought to work with colleagues to develop and offer courses in a range of disciplines through open learning. The Unit was minimally resourced and separated from the mainstream of academic provision. Not surprisingly, the Unit's impact was minimal. It is fair to say that the College did not capitalize on this early experimental initiative, as institutional emphasis by the late 1980s became focused on rapid expansion and a concentration on higher education (rather than on both further and higher education). Open learning was marginalized with only isolated pockets of continuing interest.

In the early 1990s, a re-evaluation of the institution's teaching and learning strategy led to reconsideration of open learning in the context of progress to university status. Senior management became convinced of the benefits of incorporating open learning methodologies within the institution's campus-based undergraduate provision thereby adopting the mixed-mode approach. Simultaneously, it was recognized that to adopt a production-based open learning strategy could only yield significant benefit after several years of substantial investment; in a period of rapid development, it was determined that a purchase-based strategy could yield results almost immediately. The institution, therefore, sought to utilize off-the-shelf materials obtained from a number of other institutions, most notably the Open University.

The purchased open learning materials have been used as major and essential parts of the undergraduate provision, with their use being interspersed within and beside conventional teaching. The concurrent (early 1990s) adoption of modularization for all undergraduate courses served to facilitate the adoption of open learning, since this offered an ideal opportunity to re-examine course structures and delivery methodologies. Off-the-shelf materials have been adopted from around the world and these have been subjected to the University's standard course approval and validation procedures. Furthermore, the Luton approach has provided a greater level of face-to-face support and back-up than would normally be the case for students learning at a distance.

Benefits identified from adoption of open learning materials

In taking the decision to utilize off-the-shelf open learning materials a number of factors were influential:

- The approach provided for effective use of staff resources. This was especially true in those areas of the institution which were expanding rapidly.

- Students could be provided, through the materials, with access to national and international experts in their subject.

- The accommodation pressures could be reduced since the students would be able to learn away from the University premises.

- For some students, the option of open learning enhances access to higher education. This is particularly true for the socially disadvantaged or physically disabled who might find attending on-campus courses on a full-time basis difficult.

- Open learning is a methodology increasingly adopted for in-house training by employers in all sectors of the economy. The supported use of open learning allows students the opportunity to gain competence in this approach.

- Open learning offers a strategy for reaching practitioners (such as health professionals) whose work commitments do not easily fit with conventional (part-time) attendance. Open learning allows students to learn at times convenient to themselves and not merely at times convenient to the University.

- The relative importance of the above benefits will inevitably vary over time, between academic disciplines and from student to student. At the University of Luton, experience over the past few years shows that the key feature to be taken into account is that of flexibility.

- In some cases, open learning was introduced to cope with gaps in the specialist knowledge of staff. (Tutors felt able to support the well-developed open learning packages but were less happy about developing the course themselves if it fell outside their personal expertise.) Changes to staffing may close or shift these gaps.

- It is recognized that some topics are fixed and universal features of particular disciplines nationwide or even internationally; it is for these topics that the open learning option is greatest. Other topics are of local or (relatively) short-term interest; these are less suited to open learning since the greatest flexibility is to be achieved through use of the informed individual who is able to update and revise materials in the light of developments.

Continuing developments

The Luton mixed-mode strategy was initially devised to incorporate open learning into mainstream provision. Since the early 1990s the concept has been broadened and strengthened with the inclusion of a wider portfolio of flexible learning approaches into the basic model.

- Initially, the open learning materials were selected to be able to provide sufficient content for an entire module or even multiple modules. This reflected the adoption of materials from the Open University which has, itself, a modular organization of course delivery. Increasingly, the mixed-mode approach is evolving to incorporate elements of open learning within modules rather than being the chosen mode for the module as a whole. These smaller elements can be either bought in or produced in-house to deal with particular aspects of the curriculum.

- The increasing availability of high quality computer-based materials has allowed a similar purchase strategy to be accepted. As with other forms of open learning materials, the production of computer based learning materials is expensive and is only viable if the material is to be used by a large number of students. In-house production will always be limited. The government-funded Teaching and Learning Technology Programme has yielded a wide range of materials, a selection of which are being incorporated into the Luton curriculum. However, as with other open learning materials there is a clear need to select those which fit the pedagogic needs of the institution; it is with this in mind that the University of Luton has not restricted its selection to UK sources and, for instance, is using a Canadian product for the teaching of microbiology.

- The advent of open learning required a rethink of delivery methodologies and led in time to acceptance of the concept that, in principle at least, every module could be offered by an open learning approach. A similar view has now been taken with respect to work-based learning. Thus, in principle, every programme of study could be followed by full-time or part-time attendance and could incorporate open learning and/or work-based learning. The University's modular scheme has been adapted to allow for such mixed provision.

- A full description of the development of work-based learning (WBL) would require a separate case study. However, in brief, the approach has been progressively rolled out with support from the Department for Education and Employment. The University now offers Access to Higher Education by WBL (in conjunction with local further education colleges), a single module by work-based learning (available to all students regardless of discipline) and the opportunity for a limited (but growing) range of degrees taken in WBL mode by those in full-time employment.

CONCLUSION

The adoption of a mixed-mode approach to course delivery has played a significant role in the expansion and development of the University of Luton. It has allowed the return on scarce resources to be maximized while providing students with a broader educational experience than would be the case if delivery were limited to a single mode. This broad approach equips students with skills for both employment and lifelong learning. In particular, it contributes to the ability to be an independent learner able to cope with a range of teaching and learning methodologies.

Chapter 25

Flexible Learning – Where Does the Library Fit in?

Tony Cavanagh

This case study will discuss the off-campus library delivery service provided by Deakin University to its 11,000 distance learning students, who live throughout Australia and overseas. It argues that distance students have the same right to library services as do their on-campus counterparts. The provision of a library service contributes directly to their education and facilitates flexible learning.

INTRODUCTION

Despite the increasing popularity of distance learning in recent years, there is little consensus among academic staff, distance educators and institution administrators on whether the library has a role to play in supporting distance learners. While librarians have long argued that students need library services whether they attend the campus in person or are studying hundreds of miles from their home campus, many producers of study programmes seem content to ignore the library's role, either not considering it or arguing that study packages are self-contained and include all that the student is required to know. Indeed, the recently completed survey by the University of Sheffield, England, 'The Role of the Library in Postgraduate Distance Learning', revealed confusion among course providers on the level of support they were prepared to give their students (Bolton, Unwin and Stephens, 1997) and a significant 'underestimate (of) the extent of library use required by their students' (Unwin, 1996).

Deakin University has had a strong tradition in distance learning since its formation in 1977. Prior to amalgamations in the early 1990s, around 60 per cent of its students were studying this way. Right from the outset, external students had access to a library delivery service, with books being delivered by courier with a prepaid return bag included, and with photocopies provided at no cost. From very modest beginnings (the 1250 external students made just 1479 requests in 1978), the service has grown. In 1996, over 85,000 requests were processed and 55,000 books and over 25,000 photocopies were supplied from six campus libraries.

This case study outlines the philosophy behind the library service and elaborates on reasons why we believe that access to the library is vital to students' academic and professional development. I will then describe briefly how students' request and receive material, placing emphasis on electronic access and delivery. I conclude with a suggested list of minimum standards that should apply to library services in the distance learning environment.

A PHILOSOPHY OF LIBRARY SERVICE FOR DISTANCE LEARNERS

The Deakin University Library's approach to service for distance learning students was shaped by the first University Librarian, Margaret Cameron (Cameron, 1978; 1988; Cameron and Cooper, 1972) and also by the 'Guidelines for Library Services to External Students' of the Library Association of Australia (Crocker 1982). These took as a central theme the proposition that off-campus students had the same rights to library services as did on-campus students. Translated into practice, the philosophy meant that the Library accepted responsibility for supplying books, audiovisual items and photocopies to its students, no matter where they lived. It also provided a reference service, inter-library loans for eligible students and supplied letters of introduction to enable its students to use other libraries if this was more convenient. Currently, around 40 per cent of Deakin University's 11,000 distance learners live outside the state of Victoria, including some 950 who reside overseas. The basic service philosophy espoused above is still followed today (Cavanagh and Tucker, 1997; Tucker, 1996).

From the student's point of view, the availability of a library service removes a major barrier to their study – lack of access to resources. While many are prepared to search for their own material, others do not have the time, or are physically isolated, or simply cannot locate relevant information. Furthermore, if contact with the service is made as easy as possible, if response is prompt, if satisfaction rate is high and if the students incur minimum additional costs, then students will use it. Having a library that comes to them allows learners to take responsibility for their own learning, supports their requirements for additional information for essay and thesis projects, and places their destiny into their own hands. They have the choice of obtaining supplementary material to assist them with their work or relying on their own resources.

If we assume they will prefer the former, then how might such a service operate?

THE DEAKIN UNIVERSITY LIBRARY OFF-CAMPUS SERVICE

I will describe the operation of the delivery service under these headings:

- the library collection;
- requesting material;
- delivery of material;
- reference assistance;
- the future role of electronic access.

The library collection

To obtain information on recommended reading for courses, the library maintains close contact with academic staff through liaison librarians who attend university school-board meetings and report back on new or changed academic programmes. Library staff also actively solicit reading lists from academic staff. The library has also arranged with the publishing unit of the university to provide copies of course material (study guides) at the 'galley-proof' stage for all new and re-made courses. Library staff check the references in these and order material accordingly, obtaining multiple copies of recommended and highly recommended books in proportion to the number of students in the course. Our aim is to have at least one copy of all books referred to in study guides in the library. Many courses are also offered on campus so this collection policy, which dates from the 1980s (Day and Angus, 1986; Cameron, 1988), directly benefits all students.

Requesting material

Students are given a range of options for requesting. They can order by mail, fax, telephone and e-mail; they can direct dial-in to the library catalogue and order while online; they can also order through electronic request forms on the library homepage at http://www.deakin.edu.au/library.

Electronic requesting has increased significantly in the last three years, and approximately 15 per cent of all requests are received this way. Thirty-five per cent are received by mail, 20 per cent by fax and 30 per cent by phone. Students have found dial-in access to the catalogue especially helpful for them to select their own material. Two features of the library's Innopac computer system which encourage this are 'show similar items' and 'show items nearby on shelf'. The former points the user to other books by the author(s) or items on the same subject, while the latter permits electronic 'browsing' of the shelves, literally allowing the user to check other titles on the shelf just as an on-campus student can do.

Delivery of material

Prompt delivery of requested material is also important. The library has performance standards for book and photocopy processing as follows: 90 per cent of items available for loan are despatched within 24 hours; 80 per cent of photocopies are despatched within three days of request. Delivery of books is mainly by courier within Australia and by air or courier overseas, with a pre-paid return bag included in Australia. Overseas students have their return postage refunded at the end of semester. All off-campus students make a contribution towards the cost of postage through a library delivery fee charged at time of enrolment. This is currently $A25.00 per semester within Australia and $A31.50 for overseas students. It is the only cost the student is required to make for the supply of library material.

The standard loan period for undergraduate and course work students within Australia is 12–14 days, while research students and all overseas students normally have four weeks. Books can be renewed by phone or e-mail, or by self-renewal on the library computer.

Reference assistance

Another significant need for students is that of reference assistance for help with assignments or for literature searches for a thesis or major project. Straightforward requests are handled by off-campus staff but the majority are dealt with by reference librarians. In 1996, 1900 reference requests required 955 hours of search time. Students complete a standard request form (or may telephone) and indicate any special requirements.

Reference staff make a selection from the library's holdings – books, audio visual items, journal articles, printouts from database searches or articles from full text databases – whatever they judge most appropriate. While it may appear that library staff are doing much of the student's work, the student still needs to formulate the search request and, more importantly, write the essay or thesis. The role of the library is to make the information gathering task easier for users who may not be in a position to do the work themselves.

Likewise, inter-library loans are supplied to eligible students (research and those completing a thesis or major project). There is no cost to the students but limits were applied in 1997.

Advances in communications mean that many students with modem or Internet connections can do much of their own searching. The Library's network of nearly 100 electronic databases is searchable from their terminals although some databases such as Lexis Nexis are restricted to particular categories of students. Several full-text and general purpose databases such as FirstSearch, Current Contents, UnCover, EBSCO host and Expanded Academic Index are available via telnet or web page connections and are popular with staff and students alike. Many databases run on Silverplatter ERL software and instructions for searching them, including information on searching techniques, are provided on the Library home page (http://www.deakin.edu.au/library/winspgde.html).

In addition, Library staff created a 'Research Skills' module to assist users in locating information on nearly all facets of the research process. Located at http://www.deakin.edu.au/library/reschsk.html, it has been widely publicized to off-campus students.

The future role of electronic access

Although the so-called 'electronic revolution' is often surrounded by 'hype', there is little doubt that electronic access to the Library network and the World Wide Web has made an enormous difference to the ability of distance learners to control their own learning, and partake more fully in University activities from which they are normally excluded. The recently installed software platform Interchange (http://139.132.1.5:80/div_its/interchange/frames.html) provides Deakin students with access to the Library and University networks, bulletin boards, e-mail services, computer-based conferencing, Internet tools and much more. While only around 30 per cent of our students currently have access to a modem or an Internet connection, the figure is increasing every year. I believe that the 'electronic revolution' is the greatest single factor in reducing the loneliness and isolation of the distance learner.

MINIMUM STANDARDS FOR LIBRARY SERVICES

While this case study has concentrated on the delivery service provided by Deakin University, it is not the only model which is available. In the United States, and to a lesser extent Canada, much distance education teaching is undertaken on satellite campuses at which students attend classes. In England, franchising of courses occurs although there is concern about the quality of available library services (Goodall, 1995). In both these cases, it may be more appropriate for the home institution library to provide suitable books and reserve photocopy collections to the satellite campus or franchised site. Such a system can break down when the number of courses becomes excessive or the number of sites too large, and of course it does not serve the needs of the isolated student.

Institutions need to consider providing a postal delivery service to support their distance learning students who do not have access to the home or satellite campus collection. To do this successfully the following is required:

- a commitment from the institution administration and library to fund and adequately staff the service;
- the purchase of library materials to support distance learning programmes;
- consideration of methods of access for students – mail and fax as a minimum, with phone highly desirable, even if for restricted hours daily;
- electronic access to library catalogues and databases as the ultimate aim of all services;
- free delivery of material with prepaid return bag a desirable although expensive option; courier delivery, perhaps for a fee, could also be offered;
- manageable performance standards which ensure consistent quality of service;
- provision of a reference service and an allowance for inter-library loans to eligible students;
- development of reciprocal borrowing agreements between institutions to enable students to use more convenient library access, a key desire expressed in the recent University of Sheffield survey (Bolton, Unwin and Stephens, 1997); borrowing privileges in Australian institutions can be seen at http://www.deakin.edu.au/library/borrowpriv.html.

CONCLUSION

In discussing the off-campus delivery service at Deakin University Library, I have sought to emphasize that distance learning students have the same rights to a quality library service as do on-campus students. It is the responsibility of home institutions to ensure that these students, who are *their* students, are adequately supported. Our experience shows that they will and do make extensive use of a delivery service if it is available. The keys to its success are a willingness by the institution to support and fund the library service, publicity and ease of access for students, a reliable method of delivery of material and an acceptable satisfaction rate for requests.

REFERENCES

Bolton, N; Unwin, L and Stephens, K (1997) 'The Use of Libraries by Postgraduate Distance Learning Students: Whose Responsibility?' *Open Learning*, (in press, November 1997)

Cameron, M (1978) 'Deakin is Different' *Australian Academic and Research Libraries*, 9 (4), pp. 193–8

Cameron, M (1988) '"A ful long spoon", Library Collections to Serve External Students.' *Australian Academic and Research Libraries*, 19(4), pp. 223–8

Cameron, M and Cooper, W (1972) 'Library services for external students' *A forum on External Studies, 20–24 August, 1972*, University of New England, Armidale, NSW, pp. vii–xiii

Cavanagh, A K and Tucker, J (1997) 'A Library Service to Distance Learners: What Should the Library Provide?' in Watson, E F and Jagannathan, N (eds) *Library Services for Distance Learners in the Commonwealth, a reader*, The Commonwealth of Learning, Vancouver (in press)

Crocker, C (1982) *Guidelines for Library Services to External Students*, Library Association of Australia, Sydney

Day, R and Angus, J (1986) 'Off-campus acquisitions at Deakin University Library' *Library Acquisitions: Practice and Theory*, 10(4), pp. 33–42

Goodall, D (1995) 'The impact of franchised HE courses on library and information services in FE colleges' *Journal of Further and Higher Education*, 19(3), pp. 47–62

Tucker, J (1996) 'Management Issues for Off-Campus Library Delivery Services, Particularly in a Multi-Campus Environment' in: Jacob C J (ed) *The Seventh Off Campus Library Services Conference Proceedings* Central Michigan University, Mt Pleasant, Michigan, pp. 363–73

Unwin, L (1996) 'The role of libraries in postgraduate distance learning' Paper presented to the 12th Annual CADE Conference, 22–25 May 1996, Moncton, New Brunswick

Chapter 26

Flexible Learning as a Management Issue

Patrick McGhee

In 1992 the University of Derby (then Derbyshire College of Higher Education) set up a new Division of Psychology with an educational remit to deliver high-quality, cost-effective professionally recognized degree programmes in psychology to a diverse range of undergraduates exploiting flexible learning strategies to support a student-centred approach. This philosophy was reflected in the staffing, capital investment and delivery formats adopted. This brief case study outlines strategies pursued during the first five years of operation (1992–97), including the use of educational video, the establishment of an open learning centre, and the involvement of specialist support for materials development. The central argument presented here, based on that experience, is that analyses of flexible learning implementation cannot be separated from analyses of divisional and faculty management.

INTRODUCTION

Approximately 40 per cent of students studying psychology at Derby between 1992 and 1997 were mature students, many with child care commitments, often coming to psychology as part of diverse modular combined studies programmes based on a semester system. Additionally, over the same period, the institution was particularly affected by a dwindling unit of resource starting from a base of per student funding among the worst in the UK. Nevertheless, the philosophy of the Division of Psychology proved successful in supporting the learning needs of the student groups (the dropout rate was on average less than 3 per cent). The Division adopted an 'integrationist' philosophy of delivery, combining software, video and print materials, study groups, e-mail communication and World Wide Web resources with traditional lecture, seminar and tutorial support.

The core idea around which the flexible learning strategies of the Division were integrated was a belief in the accessibility, acceptability and flexibility of educational video, in particular an innovative system developed at Derby known as 'VESOL' (Video autoEditing System for Open Learning). VESOL enables online editing of a lecture by the lecturer during the presentation itself (see O'Hagan, 1995 for a description). The videotape thus produced can be viewed by students at home, on-site in groups or alone. VESOL tapes can also be used as the primary material for clipping into TOTAL – a simple multimedia authoring program. The project was funded by a grant from the Teaching and Learning Technology Programme (McGhee, 1997).

INTEGRATED FLEXIBLE LEARNING INITIATIVES

Examples of the flexible learning approach adopted by the Division included:

- establishing an open learning centre exclusively for psychology students where paper', video and electronic resources were available in one location coordinated by a full-time manager (one of our own psychology graduates with information technology skills);

- routine recording of all year 1 and most year 2 lectures using VESOL. This created a video lecture bank of around 160 tapes freely available from the University library/learning centre. This helped students revise, catch missed sessions and sample optional modules, and reduced the tendency for verbatim note taking during live lectures;

- production of simple, customized multimedia lessons using TOTAL. This reinforced key ideas; from lectures, seminars and set texts.

- the system proved particularly effective for delivering revision exercises for two large year 1 module exams ('Introduction to Psychology' and 'Child Psychology');

- provision of entire modules in an open learning format in years 1 and 2 of the degree based on VESOL tapes and TOTAL lessons supported by study guides and surgeries. Videotapes of 1994 'Child Psychology' lectures were used as open learning material in 1995. Statistical analysis of course work and exam performance showed no difference in results achieved by students using video compared to traditional delivery modes (McGhee, 1997);

- provision of a pre-semester 'summer school' for mature students in a largely resource-based learning format;

- extensive provision of study guides in electronic as well as print format on the Internet to support open and traditional modules. These study guides enabled students to work online, e-mail staff, and search for key terms.

A number of specific challenges were presented by the modular, semesterized, combined studies framework which were directly addressed through the application of flexible methods:

- **Time tabling**

  Within a combined studies modular scheme, tight, centralized time tabling on the basis of some form of subject zoning is inevitable. VESOL permitted additional lectures to be taped and made available to all students.

- **Semester system**

  Within a modular semester scheme it can be difficult for students to build on modules taught, completed and assessed within a ten-week period the previous academic year. This lack of 'vertical integration' was addressed through summer workbooks created by staff for every autumn semester module (and some spring semester modules). These typically contained a recent key journal article with a set of brief study notes and questions. These were dispatched to the home address of every second and third year student for completion prior to the start of the semester. These articles formed the bases of the initial seminars in each module. Students welcomed these partly because of anxieties regarding the short length of the autumn teaching semester.

STAFF ISSUES

The distinctive roles of part-time and full-time staff underline the centrality of management issues for implementing effective flexible learning developments. In dealing with large first year classes the availability of specialist part-time staff to support regular weekly module surgeries and prepare first drafts of study guides was critical. The involvement of part-time staff was supported through investment by the Division in selected staff development opportunities. Additionally, part-time staff were contracted for the production of open learning materials separately from classroom teaching and were provided wherever possible with desk space and office support. However, some institutional practices complicated their contribution. For example the standard part-time teaching contract was based on 'contact hours' and expected part-time tutors to 'sign-in' when coming to teach at the institution (all betraying the bureaucratic assumption that learning happens only when there is staff-student 'contact' and that learning occurs at a specifiable place and time). These were addressed directly and ultimately resolved at a managerial level, but it was clear that bureaucratic practices lagged behind institutional teaching and learning philosophies.

Full-time staff played a crucial role in leading the flexible learning developments of the Division. The person and job specifications for new lecturers specifically emphasized the importance of skills in the management of flexible learning. After appointment, the skills and efforts of full-time staff were applied to the flexible learning approach of the Division through the incorporation of performance targets explicitly related to the production of open learning resources, negotiated as a part of the institutional annual staff appraisal and development scheme. In this way, the role of teaching was afforded equal status with research from the outset. In addition, in order to reinforce the importance of flexible learning management skills over an exclusive focus on standard lecturing techniques, a traditional 'observation of teaching' scheme was abandoned in favour of a 'delivery review' system where lecturers assembled and submitted a portfolio of examples of facilitating and managing students' learning. Fully incorporated into the formal appraisal process and supported by extensive documentation, the 'delivery review' system ensured that the management of flexible learning was seen as constitutive of, and not a distraction from, 'proper teaching'. Management issues of appraisal, line-management and prioritization cannot be separated from successful flexible learning development.

CONCLUSION

Flexible learning requires flexible management. In particular the flexible management of budgets, flexibility of staff deployment and a flexibility in working in partnership with central support departments in order to meet students' needs. If successful flexible learning presupposes removing barriers, improving access, relocating responsibility for learning, re-budgeting and exploiting central learning support expertise and resources, then it presupposes the direct involvement of divisional and faculty management. Many academically successful flexible learning initiatives probably fail organizationally due to divisional managerial indifference, incompetence or hostility. Calls for management 'support' are arguably somewhat misconceived in as much as it implies flexible learning activities are *outside of* and *separate from* management. The *organization* of learning (traditional or flexible) is fundamentally a management activity and management must take responsibility for it. Management which merely 'supports' flexible learning (usually with project rather than recurrent funding) is well placed to remove that support when resources are stretched. For flexible learning to achieve high quality outcomes, it needs to be incorporated into the *routine* operational, contractual, administrative and budgetary activities of an institution. Modular, semester-based systems in principal provide the basis for such incorporation but are not in themselves enough. What is required is a radical rethinking *of what institutions should expect of academic managers*, a rethinking which moves towards resourcing learning achievement and away from subsidizing teaching habits.

REFERENCES

McGhee, P (1997) 'Producing Video Resources for the Psychology Curriculum: An Exploration in Lecturer Autonomy' in: Radford, J; Rose, D and van der Laar, D (eds) *Innovations in Teaching Psychology* Kogan Page, London

O'Hagan, C (1995) 'Video autoEditing System for Open Learning (VESOL)' in: Percival, F (ed) *Computer Assisted and Open Access Education*, Kogan Page, London

Chapter 27

Flexible Access to Learning Resources Through Electronic Course Delivery

Philip Barker

For a variety of good reasons, there is a growing need to achieve more flexible access to teaching and learning resources. The ability to share pedagogic resources both within and between universities is of paramount importance – especially in courses that involve large numbers of disparately qualified students who have very different interests and ambitions. The development of appropriate electronic 'sharing mechanisms' is therefore very important because they can provide the basis for flexible access to (and delivery of) teaching and learning materials in a global way. This case study discusses: the movement from a paper-based Open Access Student Information Service (OASIS) to an equivalent electronic system; and, some of the advantages that can be derived from using this approach to the realization of flexible learning opportunities within a university setting.

INTRODUCTION

The advent of low-cost computer technologies, readily accessible communication systems and easy-to-use authoring environments has promoted considerable interest in the use of digital electronic media for the purposes of publication. Indeed, over the last decade there has been a considerable growth of interest in the use of electronic documents. Such documents have become an important mechanism for transmitting information from one location to another (Barker *et al.*, 1995b; Maunder, 1994). Of course, documents of this sort can vary quite considerably in their content and sophistication. They range in complexity from memos and letters through to research papers, simple electronic books and sophisticated hypermedia documents which embed many different types of modality and component (Barker, 1993a; 1993b).

According to the basic characteristics that they show, Tan (1997) has classified interactive electronic documents into three basic types: static, dynamic and living. Static documents are simply emulations of their conventional paper-based counterparts; they are unreactive and do not usually change their form. On the other hand, dynamic documents may change their form and appearance - but not their content. Documents that are dynamic and which are able to change their information content are referred to as living documents. The case study described in this paper is concerned with the use of each of these types of document to provide flexible access to teaching and learning resources within a university setting.

Obviously, there are many advantages associated with the more widespread use of electronic documents. For example, they are easier to share, update and replicate. In addition, electronic documents can be more easily distributed (at a greater speed and to a far larger audience) than can conventional publications. Of course, the cost of replication and distribution is also usually much less than is the case with resources that are based on the use of paper.

The attractive features listed above are currently being explored and exploited by a number of large international publishers. For example, in the Teesside University Licensing Project (TULIP), the publisher Elsevier is currently investigating the delivery of electronic journals to a number of academic sites in North America using computer communications networks (Zijlstra, 1994). Our own use of the Internet and campus network facilities is much more modest than that of the TULIP project. Nevertheless, the basic objective is the same: to make available electronic documents (relating to academic courses) to other universities, non-academic organizations and individual users who are interested in gaining access to them. Our work involves the computerization of an OASIS which contains large volumes of conventional paper-based course support materials.

The computerization process referred to above involves three basic research and development strands:

- the conversion of existing paper documents into electronic form;
- the creation of appropriate infrastructure and support mechanisms that will facilitate the acquisition of new documents in electronic form;

- the provision of appropriate access mechanisms to allow the retrieval and distribution of these documents to users who may be based locally (on our campus) or remotely at other institutions.

Our motivation for undertaking this work is our belief that the availability of an electronic version of our OASIS facility will improve the overall performance of the teaching staff, administrators, technicians and students involved in our courses (Barker *et al.*, 1995a).

Because of the interesting problems that are involved, the remainder of this paper discusses some of the important issues relating to the computerization of our OASIS. Particular emphasis is given to the use of electronic lectures and the development of distributed computing environments to support 'electronic course delivery'.

USING ELECTRONIC COURSE DELIVERY

The general principles involved in using Electronic Course Delivery (ECD) and the various techniques for its realization have been described in some detail elsewhere (Barker, 1997). This section therefore only summarizes our approach to the use of ECD within our own university.

ECD involves the design and development of interactive electronic resources that can be used to support teaching and learning activities by both local (campus-based) students and those who reside at (and study from) remote locations. Wherever possible, materials are designed to be re-usable in many different contexts. For example, conventional lectures that are delivered by a lecturer (in a lecture theatre) using a presentation package (such as Microsoft's PowerPoint) are later recycled for use as both self-study aids for those students who attend lectures and as distance learning resources for students who study remotely.

The recycling of electronic lecture material (and any other supporting resources) for use in the self-study contexts described above often involves the augmentation and enhancement of what was presented in a live lecture – in order to compensate for the absence of a lecturer or tutor in a self-study situation. Sometimes, in order to achieve this, the environment used to embed teaching and learning materials has to be changed. For example, although basic PowerPoint presentations can be accessed and read using a web browser such as Netscape (augmented with a 'helper' application), it is not easy to augment these presentations or embed the extra interactivity that is needed for self-study. In order to overcome these difficulties it is necessary to export the teaching/learning materials to other environments that are capable of providing the necessary facilities. In our case we export material from PowerPoint and various word-processing systems to Hypertext Mark-up Language (HTML) format (the mark-up language that forms the basis of the World Wide Web).

Once materials are in HTML format, they can be augmented and enhanced through the addition of links to other resources, the use of 'Common Gateway Interface' techniques and the incorporation of Java applets. It is also possible to add help facilities, various types of annotation and self-assessment mechanisms (to enable students to gauge the progress they are making). As well as publishing our teaching/learning resources on our own in-house intranet (the Electronic OASIS), we are also able to make these materials available publicly (via the Internet) and on CD-ROM.

EVALUATION ISSUES

An important aspect of our development work has been the assessment and evaluation of both the resources that have been produced and the mechanisms of access that we have been providing. As mentioned above, the Electronic OASIS is made available to staff and students using intranet, Internet and CD-ROM publication methods. In all cases the same basic access software is used – a Netscape browser. The enduser interfaces to the electronic course materials use familiar library, bookshelf and book metaphors. The evaluation studies that we have conducted indicate that, in general, users of our Electronic OASIS found these interfaces fairly intuitive and very easy to use (Tan, 1997). Furthermore, the consistent use of the same interface metaphors across different publication media was thought to be very helpful. Another attractive feature of the system, from both staff and student perspectives, was the built-in, automated self-assessment mechanisms that interactive electronic materials are able to provide.

Because of their importance within the context of developing supportive self-study environments, we are currently involved in an in-depth study of the ways in which different presentation modalities (text and audio) can be used to augment and enhance the basic teaching/learning resources that are held within our Electronic OASIS. A series of controlled evaluation studies is therefore being conducted (Hudson, 1997). The aim of these is to explore the relative costs of, student preferences for and pedagogic effectiveness of using different modes of augmentation and enhancement (that is, text, audio, graphics, and so on). Hopefully, the results of this investigation will not only guide us with respect to what is 'best practice' but, we anticipate that they will also inform us about the types of development tool that are needed to support this work.

CONCLUSION

There are many advantages to using electronic course delivery as a means of implementing flexible approaches to teaching and learning. However, the successful use of this technique depends upon three essential requirements:

- first, an institutional or departmental commitment to the use of interactive electronic documents for the support of teaching and learning;

- second, the provision of appropriate organisational and technical infrastructures to facilitate this approach;

- third, enthusiasm on the part of students and staff to use electronic resources within their teaching and learning activities.

Within our own department (the School of Computing and Mathematics), we have found that the Electronic OASIS which we built was enthusiastically received by both students and staff.

REFERENCES

Barker, P G (1993a) 'Authoring Hypermedia Documents' *Journal of Document and Text Management*, 1(3), pp. 191–214
Barker, P G (1993b) *Exploring Hypermedia*, Kogan Page, London
Barker, P G (1997) 'Electronic Course Delivery', special edition of *Innovations in Education and Training International*, 34(1), pp. 1–69
Barker, P G; Banerji, A K; Richards, S R and Tan, C M (1995a) 'A Global Performance Support System for Students and Staff' *Innovations in Education and Training International*, 32(1), pp. 35–44
Barker, P G; Beacham, N; Hudson, S and Tan, C M (1995b) 'Document Handling in an Electronic OASIS' *The New Review of Document and Text Management*, 1 pp. 1–17
Hudson, S R G (1997) *Multimedia Performance Support Systems* draft PhD thesis, School of Computing and Mathematics, University of Teesside, Newcastle-upon-Tyne
Maunder, C (1994) 'Documentation on Tap' *IEEE Spectrum*, 31(9) pp. 52–56
Tan, C M (1997) *Hypermedia Electronic Books* draft PhD thesis, School of Computing and Mathematics, University of Teesside, Newcastle-upon-Tyne
Zijlstra, J (1994) 'The University Licensing Programme (TULIP): A Large Scale Experiment in Bringing Electronic Journals to the Desk Top' *Serials*, 7(2) pp. 169–72

Chapter 28

An Open Learning Centre at the University of Bristol

Cathy Hole

In April 1994 the University of Bristol opened a small pilot open learning centre (OLC) on the ground floor of the main library building as part of its institution-wide information technology (IT) learning strategy (Hole, 1993).

The aims of the university in setting up the pilot centre were:

- to provide staff and students from all disciplines with a flexible means of acquiring personal, management, IT and study skills: a 'one-stop skills shop' for staff and students;

- to provide a 'show case' for the self-paced learning materials (computer, video, audio and text based) being developed within the university, by commercial organizations and by national initiatives such as the Information Technology Training Initiative (ITTI) and the Teaching and Learning Technology Programme (TLTP);

- to provide alternatives to the more traditional staff development courses, using medium as message to demonstrate to staff a range of approaches to learning and hence teaching.

The open learning centre (OLC) was funded by a small grant (£18,000) from the university's fund for innovation in teaching and learning in 1993, as a joint project between the library and the computing service. This money enabled the purchase of furniture, three personal computers (PCs), a television and video and a small collection of materials. The centre was staffed jointly by the computing service and the library.

OPEN LEARNING

The inspiration for the OLC came from visits to Hewlett Packard's open learning centre at their Bristol site. By 1993, when the idea was first discussed in the University of Bristol, the concept of open learning was well established and the benefits known (by for example the training enterprise councils (TECs) see Trusler *et al.* 1991). There was a growing interest in open learning centres in small and large businesses and in further education colleges. There was support in the form of project reports and guidelines from the (then) Department of Employment Training Agency and the TECs (see for example SCOTTSU, 1991 and THK Training, 1991). But there was little experience of open learning centres in the 'older' universities and it was not obvious that the concept would be successful in a research-based university such as Bristol.

THREE YEARS ON...

Usage and resources

Three years on the centre is well established with a good foundation of materials (over 370 items) in a variety of media (paper, audio, video, computer-based text and graphics and CD-ROM) covering a variety of skill areas. An extra personal computer (PC) has been added and the centre is now surrounded by a sea of public-access PCs on which students (and staff) can do word-processing, use electronic mail, etc. The function of the open learning support desk has been extended to become a general-help desk.

The centre is used regularly and frequently by both staff and students for their own self-paced development (with PC usage of 90–100 per cent from 12.00 noon to 18.00 weekdays in term time). After an initial slow start and a high investment of staff time to set up, monitor, evaluate and develop the OLC, it now requires little maintenance or staffing. Beaton, (1995) also reports the initial need for high investment of resources at start up.

At the start the centre's main use was by students using computer-based typing tutorials. Still popular, these have now been overtaken by Internet access, word processing tutorials and Windows tutorials. The provision of information technology skills training for students remains patchy within departments, and the OLC has provided a safety net where any student can learn about computing. In particular it has proved a popular resource for those students whose first language is not English, who have no keyboard skills and no previous computing experience. Computer-based tutorials can be infinitely patient.

Use by staff is steady, but in the main staff prefer to acquire their IT skills via the very successful programme of computing service courses. The suspicion is that some staff do not like to learn alongside students. OLC materials are however a recommended way to acquire prerequisite or follow-on skills to courses run by the computing service and the staff development department. And all new staff are introduced to the centre as part of a 'treasure hunt' within the University's induction programme.

One of the other early groups to take to the centre was the library staff. Confident with online catalogues but not with PCs, the OLC provided library staff with an opportunity to experience and learn about PCs before they arrived on their desks. The education librarian was so taken by the idea that he has set up a mini open learning centre in the education library.

Although the OLC was initially a joint project, the management and staffing have now devolved entirely to the library, but with ideas and materials provided by the University's staff development department, computing service, teaching support unit, learning technology support service (LTSS) and school of education. In fact one of the unpredicted spin-offs has been that the centre has provided a focal point and even rallying site for staff in various services with a remit or interest in open and flexible learning. It has helped to open up and focus the debate on flexible learning within the university.

The OLC now also houses a rapidly growing collection of materials on teaching and learning, flexible learning, resource-based learning etc, including a locally-written online tutorial showing how technology can be used in teaching.

Logistics

One issue which was clear from the start was that the OLC had to be staffed. Both staff and students can be easily discouraged by even the most trivial problem if there is no one on hand to put them right. So staff and students new to the centre are encouraged to come along when there is someone on duty. Initially staffed from 10.00–14.00 weekdays and now from 10.00–16.00 the centre is open as long as the library is open (up to 23.00 in term time). People seem able and happy to work on their own once they are familiar with the centre and the materials.

Paper booking-sheets, one for each workstation, provide a simple, do-it-yourself booking mechanism which has proved surprisingly successful. An earlier, online booking system was abandoned as it was a deterrent to one of the centre's main target groups, those with no keyboard or IT skills.

Putting the centre in the library was a pragmatic decision: the library was able to rearrange other facilities to create the space. Yet, I believe, this has been one of the major factors in its success. For many staff and students, the library is familiar and non-threatening and certainly less threatening than a computer laboratory. Also, there is a fine line between security and accessibility of materials. After a faltering start of too much security and hence too little use, followed by too much access and hence theft and damage, the centre has now achieved a balance. This success is largely because librarians know about the contradictions of access and security; it is an on-going problem with any library collection.

Because the centre was part of the library, almost all materials could be catalogued and made available on loan (with the exception of those computer-based courses which are only licensed for the PCs in the centre). The catalogue is of course available online throughout the University.

Siting the OLC in the library has meant that many existing resources which have been collecting dust on people's shelves or borrowed through adhoc loan systems have been pulled together and are available university-wide through a standard loan procedure. Pointers are provided to other collections of materials such as the videos and booklets on curriculum vitae and interviewing skills held by the careers advisory service.

Futures

The ideal scenario is a central file-server delivering computer-based tutorials to every PC in the library, in PC labs or on the desk of every academic in the University. But we are not quite there yet. CD-ROMs can be networked but we are not yet at the stage of networking them to every PC on campus. Many Teaching and Learning Technology Programme products have proved disappointingly difficult to port on to local file servers. Commercial suppliers are not yet at the stage of being readily able to offer site licences for their courses. Meanwhile, computing service staff are developing tools to limit access to the correct number of licensed file-served packages to the correct campus machines. The ideas are all there, the technology is not far off.

Although the centre is currently heavily used by students and some staff in a self-paced, self-motivated way, little use has been made of it or its materials by teaching staff in a structured way for students. However a follow-on project (jointly run by the computing service and school of education with three pilot academic departments) is looking at the use of open and self-paced learning for the acquisition of IT skills as a core part of the curriculum.

The OLC is developing a strategy to ensure self-paced learning can be used proactively by teaching staff throughout the university. This strategy will need input from the library, from the computing service, from staff development, from the learning technology support service, from the teaching support unit and from the school of education. But the OLC had made these links possible and it is the links which will help take the strategy and self-paced and open learning forward.

CONCLUSION

The open learning centre has shown to staff and students that flexible, self-paced learning using a variety of media is an appropriate way to acquire skills, concepts and knowledge. Its challenge now is to show that flexible, self-paced learning can be used as a core part of the curriculum right across the University.

REFERENCES

Beaton, D (1995) *The Cost-Effectiveness of Open and Flexible Learning for TECs*, Research Strategy Branch, Department of Employment, London
Hole, C J (1993) *An Information Technology Learning Strategy for the University*, University of Bristol (see URL http://www.cse.bris.ac.uk/help/docs/policies/itls.htm)
THK Training (1991) *Establishing an open learning centre*, THK Training
Trusler, A; Martucci, J and Connell, T (1991) *Open Learning: a Guide to Good Practice* Department of Employment, Training, Enterprise and Education Directorate, Leeds
SCOTTSU International Limited (1991) *Establishing Quality Flexible Learning Resource Centres: Project Report* SCOTTSU International Limited, Scotland

Chapter 29

Staff Development for Flexible Learning at Stockport College

Jackie Robinson

Stockport College of Further and Higher Education is in a relatively unique position in the education sector as it provides flexible learning programmes which span both the further and higher education curriculum. This reflects the range of work that the college itself provides, with education and training programmes available at all levels from pre-GCSE to degree. We are a University College of the University of Manchester but we also work in partnership with a number of other universities for our higher education level provision.

Flexible Learning Services was established in the college in 1987. Each year since then the service has grown and diversified. During the 1995-96 academic year there were almost 4000 enrolments on flexible learning programmes. This makes us one of the largest providers of flexible learning programmes in the United Kingdom. One of the unique features of the service is the wide range of types and levels of courses available – from basic numeracy, to customer service, to nine different modern foreign languages and on to professional level accountancy.

WHY IS STAFF DEVELOPMENT NEEDED?

Flexible Learning Services at the college is truly both a *year round* and *flexible* service. The Flexible Learning Centre is open 51 weeks per year, closing only for the week between Christmas and New Year. Students may enrol at literally any point in the year. There are no fixed start dates and the only restrictions on finish dates are those which may be imposed by external accreditation bodies.

The downside of such a high degree of flexibility is that there are far more opportunities for things to go wrong than on traditionally taught programmes. These are just a few of the issues that we face:

- How can we be sure that all potential students are given the same level of pre-enrolment advice and guidance throughout the year?
- How can we track and monitor the progress of students who may be coming in to college at most for half an hour per month?
- How can we be sure that students learning at a distance are achieving the learning outcomes for a particular programme?
- How will a good classroom teacher adapt to tutoring individual flexible learners?
- How will we know which learning materials will best support a particular flexible learning programme?

HOW DO WE DELIVER QUALITY?

At Stockport College, Flexible Learning Services operates strict quality procedures and systems. These incorporate a range of performance indicators to enable us to monitor service delivery year on year. These include numbers of enquiries, advice sessions and enrolments, achievement rates and withdrawal rates. The withdrawal rate is consistently between five and ten per cent. One key quality assurance activity within the service is the provision of structured staff development for all tutors. With more than 80 tutors it is vital that staff development and training has a high priority. It is not sufficient to simply provide one-off 'injections' of staff development. For most flexible learning tutors the methodology is as new as it is for the students themselves. Tutors therefore need to be provided with on-going support and development.

WHAT TYPE OF STAFF DEVELOPMENT IS NEEDED?

There are four key themes for staff development activities:

Tutor skills

Without doubt the greatest demand is in the area of the development of tutor skills. The change in role from traditional teacher to flexible learning tutor must never be underestimated. The emphasis in these sessions tends to be in examining how flexible learners will be learning differently from traditional learners and thus what this means in terms of the skills the tutor needs to effectively support them.

Learning materials

The second key area focuses on issues related to learning materials. This includes where to find specialist flexible learning materials; how to evaluate them; how to adapt existing materials; and how to write materials from scratch.

Learning technologies

Increasingly, staff development activities need to include aspects of how learning technologies may be used in flexible learning programmes either to *deliver* parts of the curriculum or to *support* learners.

Curriculum development

As pressure increases in all educational establishments to effectively do more for less, we have experienced an increase in requests from programme teams to assist with curriculum development in identifying how elements of courses may be taught more flexibly and thus reduce the amount of class contact time required.

The above is by no means a definitive list. Other topics include:

- what is flexible learning?
- administering flexible learning programmes;
- managing flexible learning programmes;
- ensuring quality in flexible learning;
- marketing flexible learning;
- flexible learning in the global context.

HOW WE PROVIDE STAFF DEVELOPMENT

At Stockport College we have four main approaches to the provision of staff development:

- The College runs a Certificate of Education programme for teachers in further, adult and higher education validated by the University of Manchester. As part of this modular programme we have a higher level module in flexible learning. This operates on a part-time day or evening basis over five weeks and covers many of the issues identified in the previous section. This programme is open to our own staff and to external teachers and trainers. It has proved to be an extremely effective vehicle for raising awareness of the issues surrounding flexible learning and helping teachers to decide whether flexible learning is appropriate for them and their programmes.

- Inevitably, with a service our size and with the continual introduction of new programmes, new staff join the Flexible Learning Services team and the College in general at different times of the year and wish to find out more about flexible learning. To cater for this we have a rolling programme of termly, half-day skills development workshops on focused topics such as an introduction to flexible learning; tutor skills; finding and evaluating learning materials; and writing flexible learning materials. These tend to be for small groups of no more than ten participants and take place in the Flexible Learning Centre to allow staff to become familiar with the centre.

- Our model of flexible learning is an integrated model within the College structure. This means that our tutors are drawn not only from part-time staff but also from full-time staff with a partial timetable commitment to flexible learning. This has encouraged the acceptance of flexible learning across the College. Even programme areas which do not currently offer their courses on a flexible learning basis make use of our staff development services, particularly in customizing a programme for specific curriculum teams who are exploring the introduction of flexible learning. This may take the form of a flexible learning 'expert' joining their planning team to assist them in considering the issues surrounding their flexibility initiatives and help them find solutions to possible problems, or providing a series of more formal staff development events similar to those outlined above but drawing solely upon examples from that curriculum area.

- With a large flexible learning portfolio, very specific staff development needs arise. For example, Student A has failed module four and needs to concentrate specifically on that for the next exam sitting – are there some alternative learning materials I could direct her to? Course Y has only recruited six students, we don't want to lose them so we'd like to 'transform' them into flexible learning students – can you help with tutor skills and materials to support this? Student B will be working abroad for the next five months and wants to continue studying completely at a distance – how can I support that student differently now that we can't meet each month to discuss problems? All of these queries are hypothetical but typical of the myriad of questions and potential need for support that tutors have. Hence we have a programmes coordinator who is an academic member of staff whose role it is to provide this kind of ongoing support to all tutors. The nature of this support may vary from pointing them in the right direction to find additional learning materials in the first example; to providing a structured skills development session in the second example; to sitting down with the tutor and discussing alternative ways of supporting distance learners in the last example.

CONCLUSION

It's an old but true adage that quality does not just happen but has to be planned for and meticulously implemented. This most definitely extends to the development of the skills needed by staff to effectively support flexible learners and I would include in the notion of 'support' not just tutorial staff but all staff involved. Institutional strategies are needed to ensure that this staff development is available throughout the year and at all levels – as indeed the flexible learning programmes are themselves.

Chapter 30

Establishing Flexible Learning in a Conventional Institution – Getting the Strategy Right

Sally Anderson

Napier University achieved university status in 1992, and has grown to become a major Scottish university with over 11,000 students. Like other higher education institutions in the United Kingdom, Napier is being encouraged by a number of factors to offer courses in a more flexible way. These factors include: restricted funding by government; government emphasis on new technologies as a way forward; the university's desire to encourage students' participation in and responsibility for their learning; the development of the concept of lifelong learning and interest in continuing professional development; widening of access to 'non-traditional' students and making study opportunities available to students with other commitments. It is in this context that Napier decided to introduce flexible learning across the university.

FLEXIBLE LEARNING AT NAPIER

A programme of development in open and flexible learning was established within the university's Educational Development Unit (EDU), and flexible learning became a notable feature of Napier's current strategic plan. However, at the principal's conference in 1995, staff contributions emphasized that no formal policy existed within which departments could work towards contributing to the strategy. Subsequently, the concept of flexible learning has gone through two stages: formal policy development and implementation.

We will explore each of these phases separately, and try and identify the enabling and inhibiting mechanisms at work during the process.

POLICY DEVELOPMENT

It was important in developing the policy that as much of the university experience as possible should be harnessed. It was also felt very strongly that all academic and relevant support departments should have input and ownership of the policy. For this reason the university committee structure seemed the most enabling one, and wherever possible the policy development followed a collegial process. At a residential away-day for senior university management the principal requested that a subcommittee be set up to find a way to take flexible learning forward. Thus began the collegial process that culminated in representation of faculties and support departments in the policy-making subcommittee.

The first crucial task for this group was to develop a working definition of what flexible learning actually meant within Napier's vision. After looking at various descriptions of open, flexible and distance learning a brief statement was drawn up denoting Napier's view:

> We have taken flexible learning to mean a combination of the best of an open attitude to learning, combined with the best of distance learning techniques and more traditional face-to-face delivery, allowing even the students who are not at a distance from their tutors to experience the convenience of not always having to learn in a time and place dependent way, but also giving the motivational assistance and support of regular tutorials and contact with peers. (Napier University Flexible Learning Policy Statement, 1996)

After a number of meetings and consultation with university staff by representatives on the subcommittee, a policy proposal was drawn up and submitted to the Central Executive Group (CEG) for approval.

This policy statement was then circulated to all deans and heads of department for discussion with staff. Wherever possible, personal discussions were held with heads of departments. This information was taken into account when drawing up a proposed implementation plan which, after a number of redrafts, was also presented to CEG for approval.

Inhibiting mechanisms

The most notable weakness in the attempt to negotiate a truly collegial policy paper was in the communication lines. Although there was representation of most groups through heads of departments, deans or other staff, some departments felt that they had not been kept well briefed on the process of the document. In addition, the very strong departmental structure made it difficult to find out exactly what pockets of experience there were in flexible learning, as there are very few fora in which this sort of information is pooled. Inevitably, some people felt that they had not been consulted.

Enabling mechanisms

It was useful to have someone on the policy development committee group who had a broad advisory remit to the principal and university management, but was not a member of the permanent academic or support staff. This advisor helped to raise difficult issues and defuse tensions because he was less embroiled in the day-to-day detail of current university activities.

Other structures which helped were information-gathering and disseminating structures, especially those which did not have particular academic allegiances. An example of this was an open session organized by the EDU called 'Food for Thought'. This was a meeting over sandwiches and coffee, which any interested staff could attend. One of these was held on flexible learning, and helped to gather opinions on the policy, and also to pool experience from various departments.

POLICY IMPLEMENTATION

In order to embed the policy in university practice, there is a need for a critical mass of support. One of the most important ingredients here is simply enough time for the re-educative process to take place. People or groups who have already embraced the idea are prepared to move swiftly to the next step, on the basis of what they believe to be a rational, empirical approach. However, others may not yet be convinced and frustration and tension between the two viewpoints results.

At Napier, the first step in implementing the flexible learning policy was a strong steer from the leadership. The vehicle used was the principal's conference. The 1996 conference focused on three particular areas of university activity, with flexible learning being one of them. The next step was university commitment to setting up infrastructure to support departmental activities by agreeing to fund a suitable level of staffing. Finally, guidelines to developing and costing flexible learning provision, including what is expected as the development progresses through the standard university planning and validation procedures, have been drawn up and are being negotiated with deans of faculties and other interested parties. Department heads are now expected to include flexible learning developments in their annual plans and longer term strategies.

Inhibiting mechanisms

The desire to maintain departmental ownership over projects and to preserve the collegial approach adopted to the policy development has led to some difficulty. The fact that modularization has not been fully implemented means that staff think first of converting whole courses of study, rather than aiming for the conversion of certain modules or even pieces of modules. In addition, the fact that the modularization system is also undergoing change places additional burdens on staff time.

It is only very recently that deans have taken direct line responsibility for the heads of department within their faculty. This role is still evolving and therefore the need for strong leadership and persuasive skills from the deans is heightened.

The strategic planning process of the university does not as yet have a very well developed implementation phase attached to it. There is not always routine follow-up on achievement of what has been put forward in these plans, which makes it difficult to see whether departments are actually fulfilling their obligations as laid down in the policy statement.

Enabling mechanisms

The principal's conference has shown itself to be a valuable collegial forum which in many ways sets up an acceptable environment for the more bureaucratic processes that may later become necessary.

The university strategic plan and the newly established flexible learning policy give some coherence to the goal of the organization. These shared goals provide an important framework within which departments can begin to expand their activities in flexible learning.

In introducing a new way of teaching, it is important that staff development activities emphasize the educational benefits and also handle sensitively people's discomfort with change, as well as acknowledging the value of previous ways of doing things. A department such as the EDU, which is seen to be politically neutral, is also the university's mechanism for filtering information from outside the institution and presenting valuable ideas to academic departments for consideration. The EDU is a centre of expertise on teaching and learning, and the credibility to play this role. It also provides an environment in which new and different activities and ideas can be tested and piloted, without damaging the credibility of the persons and department involved, or the standing of the university. This kind of structure is needed, particularly in an unstable environment where a lot of external changes and information require processing.

It has been pointed out that in order to introduce change in any organization strong leadership is needed at all levels. This is certainly becoming clear as interest in flexible learning expands, with strong proponents needed from the level of principal, through assistant principals, deans, heads of departments, course leaders and individual lecturers who are not only open to new approaches, but are also willing to share their experiences with each other.

CONCLUSION

At Napier, it was felt that if flexible learning was to become a core of the teaching and learning strategy of the university, it had to be shifted from a kind of 'cottage industry' to a formal, institutional initiative. This vision is being realized by the introduction of a widely negotiated and distributed flexible learning policy statement, and an implementation plan which has the support of senior management and senior academic staff and the dedicated effort of a flexible learning team. It is hoped that this will lay the foundation for confident planning and development and ownership of flexible learning initiatives by all academic departments in the university.

Chapter 31

The Flexible Learning Initiative at Loughborough University

Winnie Wade

The Flexible Learning Initiative (FLI) contributes to the development of effective and efficient quality teaching across campus through:

- the provision of advice on flexible learning;
- developing student independence in learning through the provision of study support;
- establishing and supporting flexible learning development projects across campus;
- promoting the use of technology in teaching and learning;
- disseminating information about flexible learning both internally and externally;
- evaluating the effectiveness of teaching and learning strategies.

Through our continuing education work we are also extending our support to part-time students in business and industry who are undertaking study at Loughborough University.

BACKGROUND

In 1992 the former Universities Funding Council initiated a programme to encourage flexibility in course provision. The purpose of this programme was to promote the development of more flexible patterns of teaching and learning and a review of the content and structure of courses. Support was provided for 28 varied projects at 22 higher education institutions under the Flexibility in Course Provision (FCP) programme. One of these projects, the FLI, was based at Loughborough University. Loughborough's grant was supported and augmented by the university and in 1993, a full-time flexible learning coordinator was appointed to manage the initiative.

Loughborough University is committed to the development of innovative strategies for teaching and learning. To this end the university established the FLI with a broad remit to support such innovation on a variety of levels throughout the institution. The strategic plan clearly identifies the university's commitment to flexible learning. 'The University will aim to be at the forefront of developments in flexible learning generally as part of its commitment to a student-centred learning culture and in recognition of the increasing diversity of student learning needs' (Strategic Plan, 1995). In the first year, a number of projects were established within the initiative across the range of academic departments, developing a wide variety of flexible learning strategies. As a result of these projects (for more details refer to Wade *et al.* (1994)), a wider range of learning opportunities was provided for the students with a broader repertoire of teaching strategies in use by staff.

The FLI is now a well established central support unit at the University and fundamental to the strategic aim of supporting student-centred learning.

THE WORK OF THE FLEXIBLE LEARNING INITIATIVE

The FLI is the principal focus of the university's innovations in the delivery of courses to students and is the centre for teaching and learning support at Loughborough University.

The FLI is committed to student-centred teaching and learning and provides an environment which facilitates student involvement in the learning process. This flexible learning approach recognizes the need to maintain and enhance teaching quality at a time of rapidly increasing student numbers with an increasingly diverse student population.

The FLI has a campus-wide role in the strategic development of teaching and learning, offering a comprehensive support service to staff which involves expert consultancy, project funding, the provision of developmental workshops and the production of resource materials. It works at all levels within the institution to achieve its objectives, regularly collaborating with members of senior management, faculty and departmental representatives, other academic support services and student groups.

There are a number of interlinked aspects to the work of the FLI:

- support of innovative teaching and learning projects;
- computer assisted learning;
- study skills provision;
- continuing education;
- computer assisted assessment support;
- distance learning.

Support of innovative teaching and learning projects

The FLI works in collaboration with academic and service departments on campus on specific projects aimed at enhancing the teaching and learning experience for Loughborough students.

Computer assisted learning (CAL)

Responsibility for the implementation of CAL at Loughborough lies with the FLI.

The work involves:

- liaison with every department to establish where the introduction of CAL would be beneficial;
- liaison with Computing Services to ensure that the demands of CAL materials can be met;
- collecting together materials as they become available, testing them and configuring them for network use;
- matching the materials to individual course modules so that each member of staff only evaluates materials relevant to the topics they teach
- setting up and maintaining a server dedicated to CAL materials and accessible from every computer on campus;
- writing custom software to access the new teaching materials;
- ensuring that all computer labs are of equivalent configuration and can handle the new materials.

The FLI currently supports over 160 different CAL packages from more than 30 different sources. In addition, the initiative has a leading role in several CAL-based projects at Loughborough. These will produce customized packages, tailored to the needs of our courses.

Study skills provision

The FLI offers a comprehensive study skills programme for all undergraduate students. This responsibility was a natural development as study skills underpin all aspects of teaching and learning. The study skills programme involves the distribution of the Loughborough University Study Guide and Information Technology Skills Guide to first year students, the provision of study workshops promoting skills development and discussion, and the development of materials for academic staff to use in their teaching. The Study Guide is a comprehensive guide to studying in higher education. It provides detailed advice on a variety of study techniques from examination revision to making oral presentations. A companion to the Study Guide is the IT Skills Guide which is a comprehensive guide to the IT facilities at Loughborough and introduces students to basic IT skills. A range of study workshops are organized for students which assist with study skills methods. Study advice sheets give information about study skills and cover a broad range of study areas.

The FLI is also working with many of the university's academic departments to incorporate study advice, support and direct training in key skill areas within a department's teaching methods. Material is being targeted towards specialized subject areas so that students receive the support they need to carry out their particular course work requirements.

Continuing education

Loughborough University has a substantial reputation for its continuing vocational education provision for industry and the professions. It has recently reorganized the structure of its support service in this area by creating a new post of continuing education coordinator. This post is attached to the FLI.

Our current role in Continuing Education is to provide central support for all departments in the university to develop initiatives which will provide wider access to study and certification, be responsive to the demands of industry and commerce, enhance the personal and vocational development of professionals in all walks of life and, where possible, to make effective use of flexible learning systems and technologies to achieve these aims.

Computer assisted assessment support

Computer Assisted Assessment (CAA) Support is supported by the University's Special Initiative Funding and is coordinated by the FLI. The aims of the project are to advise, encourage and enable individual members of academic staff to implement methods of computer-assisted assessment on campus, if these are felt to be appropriate as part of the teaching and learning experiences on the modules in which they are involved. The impetus for wider-scale use of CAA has come from a combination of the following factors:

- the need to teach and assess increasing numbers of students with no corresponding increase in resources;
- the increasing diversity of backgrounds of incoming students;
- the development of user friendly commercial authoring packages enabling the relatively easy creation of assessment tests;
- the availability of computer terminals in higher education institutions for student use;
- the demand for more flexible delivery of material to students and introduction of CAL materials.

The principal methods of CAA being developed by the project are:

- the use of the optical mark reader to mark multiple choice question tests;
- the delivery of computer-based tests and exercises over the university computer network including the use of World Wide Web technology.

In addition to this development work, activities promoting the project's aims include workshops on topics of relevance, individual consultations with interested academic staff, the authoring of tests in Question Mark Designer software for individual members of academic staff, the production of printed guides to CAA procedures at Loughborough University, and the dissemination of information throughout the campus.

Distance learning

The FLI is coordinating a university-wide initiative to develop distance learning materials for external clients.
The project aims to:

- develop computer-based learning materials for delivery at a distance;
- record and report upon the development process;
- establish a prototype delivery infrastructure;
- evaluate the pedagogic effectiveness of prototype courseware;

- investigate the value and efficiency of a variety of tools, techniques and delivery formats.

CONCLUSION

The success of the FLI has depended upon its coordinated approach to teaching and learning innovation rather than an *ad hoc*, piecemeal approach. Strong institutional support for the FLI at a senior level has encouraged more widespread innovation. It has been important to develop a strategic approach to teaching and learning which provides mechanisms which enable staff to maintain and improve the quality of the teaching process. The provision of learning support for students at an institutional level has also been a significant factor in this strategic approach. As it is unlikely that pressure on resources will diminish, the work of the FLI will become even more important in an ever uncertain future in higher education.

REFERENCES

Wade, W B; Hodgkinson, K; Smith, A and Arfield, J (eds) (1994) *Flexible Learning in Higher Education*, Kogan Page, London

Conclusion

This collection of case studies paints a broad picture of flexible learning developments in higher education in the United Kingdom, Australia and the United States of America. It reveals that higher education institutions in these countries are facing very similar pressures to increase the amount of flexibility in their courses. It also reveals that flexible approaches to teaching and learning are being adopted in all subject areas, and that many approaches are transferable from one discipline to another.

A number of trends concerning the introduction of flexible learning have emerged from the case studies:

- The introduction of more flexible delivery methods is resulting in a blurring of the distinction between 'traditional' campus-based learners and distance learners.

- A number of higher education institutions are developing integrated strategies for supporting remote and campus-based students.

- Many flexible learning innovations for campus-based students remain at the module or unit level.

- The needs of many work-based learners are being met by a growing number of purpose designed distance learning courses which support and develop the reflective practitioner.

- An important element of flexibility for work-based learners is the opportunity to negotiate entry and exit points, pace, content, and assessment to suit their work situation.

- Flexible delivery methods are enabling higher education institutions to target new markets. Whilst some distance learning courses have made this goal explicit (Northern College, Scotland, have marketed the Diploma in Applied Studies in Education and Training internationally, Chapter 15) for others, this has been more of an unplanned benefit.

- In almost all the case studies, the relationship between the student and the tutor has involved the students being actively responsible for their own learning, with the tutor acting as a facilitator of this learning.

- Only a few case studies have actively addressed the staff development implications of this new role for tutors, although several case studies have addressed the need to develop students' skills for lifelong learning, whether at foundation level or postgraduate level.

- Some students are ill at ease with the amount of responsibility given to them in flexible learning situations. A large proportion of the case studies refer to the importance of student support. For example, Cock and Pickard (Chapter 16) state that 'undoubtedly some students were not at ease with the amount of responsibility given to them and wanted the comfort of lectures'. Fulkerth (Chapter 1) points out that students 'who are not able to work alone, or who are not highly motivated' require a great deal of support.

- Higher education institutions are finding it necessary to adopt flexible learning approaches to the development of students' transferable skills. This indicates that more 'traditional' forms of delivery are proving inappropriate for developing skills for a diverse student population.

- A number of institutions are taking a strategic approach to supporting flexible learning, either across the whole institution or within a department. The experience at Luton University, England (Chapter 24), would imply that initiatives will remain 'experimental' and so marginalized if senior management does not make a commitment to more flexible delivery at the institutional level.

- Institutional mechanisms are needed to maintain and improve the quality of flexible learning provision. As Patrick McGhee states, 'For flexible learning to achieve high quality outcomes, it needs to be incorporated into the *routine* operational, contractual, administrative and budgetary activities of an institution' (Chapter 26).

- A number of institutional and departmental strategies are being explored for encouraging more flexible approaches to teaching and learning, eg using the appraisal process to focus on a range of delivery methods rather than just on classroom observation; introducing staff development for flexible learning tutors; changing person specifications for posts providing flexible learning support so that the focus is not just on contact time; new roles for library staff who now actively support student learning; and guidelines to the development and costing of flexible learning provision.

- Some flexible learning initiatives involve the use of information and communication technologies such as e-mail, computer conferencing and the World Wide Web. There is some evidence that successful individual initiatives are leading to the development of departmental and institutional strategies for online course delivery, eg the electronic Open Access Student Information System at the University of Teesside, England (Chapter 27), and the Cybercampus at the Golden Gate University, United States of America (Chapter 1).

This edited collection illustrates the richness of approaches to flexible learning currently taking place in higher education. It shows that flexible learning is achieved by designing and delivering courses in ways which meet student needs and may involve any methods of teaching and learning to do so. A realistic approach to flexible learning initiatives must take into consideration the constraints of these resource-lean times. Initiatives are likely to be planned from a range of perspectives, including student-centred, teacher-centred and institution-centred ones. But in all cases, the aim should be to provide a flexible framework in which learning can take place with the overarching aim of meeting student needs.

Index

access 3, 16, 52, 101, 107, 110, 114, 117

accreditation 56

action learning 75

action research 74–6

active learning 4

adult learners 13, 113

APEL 81

APL 53, 61

assessment 70, 102, 125

audio 23

benchmarking 105

bulletin boards 12, 157

business writing 11-16,

campus–based 6, 10, 99, 141, 147–8, 167, 191

CD-ROM 26, 96

chemistry 44–8

choice 4, 22, 80

club management 51

community education 61, 113

computer aided assessment (CAA) 187–9

computer assisted learning (CAL) 187

computer conferencing 157

competencies 52

confidence building 50, 101

contact time 20

continuing education 61, 80, 188

continuing professional development 61, 80

control 3, 73

core skills 105, 107

curriculum development 143

Cybercampus 192

databases 132

deep approach 19

distance education 53, 143

distance learning 2, 23, 56, 61, 83, 91, 148, 153–9, 167, 187, 191

drivers 4

education studies 17, 178

e-mail 12, 14, 34–9, 42, 98, 119, 138, 157

empowerment 16, 28, 73, 77

engineering 130